# VOICES and VISIONS

# VOICES and VISIONS

## A CELEBRATION OF

## NORWICH MARKET

Joyce Dunbar
and others

Illustrations by Lys Flowerday

For JOHN AVES, 1951–2004

Voices and Visions

First published in 2005 by

Mousehold Press
Victoria Cottage
Constitution Opening
Norwich, NR3 4BD
www.mousehold-press.co.uk

Designed by Gerry Downes

ISBN 1 874739 35 8


Printed by Barnwells, Aylsham, Norfolk

CONTENTS

FOREWORD

AFTERWORD

I offer special thanks to the following people:

For details of Court records, to Colin Howey and David Tong (formerly, Tangle and Hump, Pedlars of the Past).

To my daughter Polly for transforming my story-stall and for her faith in the enterprise.

To the many artists who have contributed work for an exhibition on the theme of the market.

In a year during which the future of Norwich Market has been the subject of much debate, to the Inner City Forum for throwing open the debate, to Mark Oxley for his valuable contribution to that debate and to the Eastern Daily Press and the Evening News for their vigorous and entertaining public campaign in support of the market. To Rowan Mantell for her interested support at crucial times.

To Pat Moon for a thoughtful reading of the first draft of this book, and to Gareth Butcher for an amused reading of the second draft.

To those traders who went out of their way to encourage me when I sat in hopeful anticipation in my story-stall, including Gareth Butcher and Andy Worman. To Kevin Greene, the market manager, for giving generously of his time and knowledge.

Last, but not least, to Magdalen Russell, whose inspired idea this was.


The publishers would like to thank the Editors of the Eastern Daily Press and the Evening News for kindly granting permission to reprint copyright material in this book.

We would also like to thank Norwich City Council for their generous provision of a grant to support the publication of this book.

NORWICH
City Council

Photographic credits

The publishers would like to thank the following for providing the photographs: Alan Childs: p.15, p.20, p.33, p.58, p.66, p.80, p.82; Joyce Dunbar: p.17, p.48; Sue Mullard: p.16, p.34, p.35, p.39, p.44, p.52, p.84; Janet Watson: p.19, p.40, p.105, back cover.

This book is the result of my time as Writer in Residence on Norwich Market, officially for two days a week in the months of October, November and December 2000. The idea for the residency came from Magdalen Russell, who was running Wordwaves, for the Literature in Norfolk project, as part of the Norfolk and Norwich Festival.

Unofficially it has taken much longer. I needed time to assimilate the material I had gathered and to see how it might best be presented. But now the market is faced with imminent and possibly drastic change. As best I can, I hope to give a record of the market as it was at that time, with small additions made up to May 2004.

I took a literal stance on the residency – with the help of my daughter I turned my story-stall into a sitting-room. I had a painted fireplace, mantelpiece, window with curtains and pot plants, giant ginger cat, a picture saying 'Home Sweet Home', a coffee table and two rocking-chairs. This didn't quite work as I intended: people took me for a fortune teller.

But, bizarrely, all kinds of people did step into my stall and take a seat. They told me all kinds of things. I began to wonder what strange psychological purpose was being served, and whether the stall should be a permanent fixture (though not with me as the listener).

**I met up with my partner outside Dixons. She had been pootling on the market. I asked her what she had found there. She said there was a writer in residence. I grinned so big. My jaw just about touched the floor. Sure enough! Only a city like Norwich could do this. An open and friendly space where nothing is being sold. Where anyone can go and make the air feel richer, clearer, brighter, by sharing an experience, a feeling, an idea. Fantastic! Norwich should keep the sun shining and the clouds moving in this way. *Luke***

**What a good idea. A stall where everyone can come and sit down and write their thoughts and laments. Very therapeutic. *Diana.***

What I have written is not a history. That has been excellently done by Ursula Priestley (*The Great Market*, Centre of East Anglian Studies, 1987); neither is it a systematic or comprehensive survey. It is just one interested person's garnering. When I look at old pictures of the market, by Cotman and others, they are usually a view from a distance. I always want to home in on individuals – their faces, expressions. And then I want to hear their voices, know their thoughts. Court records afford some such glimpses.

In 1600 Helen Simpson and Ann Appleton were heard arguing in the marketplace. According to witnesses, Helen shouted 'with great anger and malice' that Ann was a 'filthie baggage' and that she would 'hold the carnal use of her body to any man'.

On another occasion, also in 1600, Henry Boyle, during an argument with Richard Carlton on Norwich market, was heard to say, 'Carlton, I know thee well enough. Thou art a drunken rascal and a paltring knave.'

More scatologically, a man threatened someone by saying, 'if he had a turd in his hand he would give him leave to chew it with his teeth'.

Gesture has the same stark eloquence. In 1621 Margaret Caly appeared before Norwich Mayor's Court because she did 'revile and miscall Christopher Giles and often times clapped her hand on her backside and bade him kiss there'.

It is here, in the momentary visions of snatched words and fleeting gesture, that people come most vividly to life. This is where my focus has been.

In the process other questions emerged to be explored. What does the market mean to the people who work there and buy there? And what about all those on the perimeter, the pavement artists, performers, beggars? There are as many answers as people. The result is a patchwork, a kaleidoscope, as random as the market itself.

Because I want to catch it as part of a living fabric rather than historical fact, much of this story is told in voices other than my own. Of course, the material is circumscribed by the people who were willing to talk to me. Some had much to say and were very eloquent. Some not so much. Others were indifferent or hostile.

The gift of a residency to a writer is that it gives special access, permission to enquire. To those who responded I give my thanks. To those not included, who would like to have been, my apologies. There are sure to be sins and omissions. I wanted to write it all: buyers and sellers, night and day, insiders and outsiders. That wasn't possible. My task was to take the shreds and patches I was able to gather, and weave them into some kind of whole.

If I have captured some of the spirit of this vibrant community, its variety and vitality, its buzz and its hum, its hubbub of personalities, then I have done what I set out to achieve.

*Joyce Dunbar, May 2004*

## Norwich Market

Grid-locked narrow passages of
claustrophobic striped tarpaulins
stretched across scaffold poles.
Hoover parts which don't quite match –
but Vax-compatible love,
and cheaper too.

Labyrinthine tunnels –
a rat run game of 90° turns;
revelations of treasure and trash,
idle browsing of old CDs
and tannin-soft blockbusters.
Cheeses of goat, and milk of ewe,
shot through with copper blue;
and indigo ceramic bells from a Norfolk
craftswoman
who calls from a map too far to travel to.
Clothes so cheap they cost coins,
collecting in zipped pockets of an apron.

The front row of the stalls watch from beneath
their tree,
leafy refugee from a London park,
huge umbrella in the event of inclement weather –
critical winos eating chips with their children,
while a torrent of taxis erode
a channel between the crowd.

The side-shows ply their wares –
fish-freshness,
black bollards and trampled flowers,
entwined in a border of pigeons,
dancing and prancing,
Big Issues flying,
sing for your supper,
Roxy's Toolbox
and change chinking into the open violin case
while the trick cyclist
clowns like a panniered paramedic.

A market's a market,
rising up
like a skate-boarding slope;
up the steps of rained-on guano,
past damp benches and greasy papers,
towards the patriarchal town hall –
blank and blind,
but with a golden clock.

*Kate Pannett*

**'You find yourself in the middle of a film, a fair, a carousel, a fairy-tale. Something from the Middle Ages.'**

Norwich Market has existed on its present site in the City Centre for almost a thousand years. It's brightly coloured striped canopies have become a trademark for Norwich. It is the largest market in England, and the only permanent market to be open six days a week, every week of the year. In the run up to Christmas many of the stalls are open seven days a week. The eighteenth-century historian, Frances Bloomfield, described it as 'the greatest market in all England'. It is rightly celebrated.

**Out of every 100 tourists, 40 visit the Cathedral, 60 go to the Castle, 80 to the Mall. But 100 come to the Market. The people in Norwich take it for granted, but the tourists think it is the most wonderful, the most attractive, the most enjoyable place to spend a couple of hours. We're the heart in the body of Norwich, pumping away.** *Joe Silvester, Pet Accessories*

First, the setting: on Gaol Hill is the beautiful old Guildhall, its lacy stonework and patterned flints a reminder of the values of another age. Opposite is the imposing Church of St Peter Mancroft, now juxtaposed to the futuristic hangar of the new Millennium Library. At the intersection of Pudding Lane and Weaver's Way is the Sir Garnet Wolsey, a traditional gabled pub with bay windows. Overlooking all, with its Acropolictic aspirations and guardian lions, is the 1930's City Hall. Standing on the steps here, looking over the striped sea of canopies, Davey Place leads directly to the ancient mound crowned by the old Norman Castle. In between is Gentleman's Walk and a row of banks, high street shops, and the beautiful Victorian arcade.

So Church, State, Government, Commerce. The imposing ranks of Law and Order. And in its midst, cradled almost, a huddle of coloured cabins, a shanty town of crooked sinks and flapping awnings, tin chimney-pots, corrugated-plastic coverings, improvised over the years by succeeding generations of stall-holders, is the ancient market.

**We're not shut away in our own little world. The world comes to us. We see everything in action. The police, the ambulances, the paper-sellers. How many people have that? And look at the wonderful buildings all around. Look! Look at them all! Peter Mancroft. Beautiful, magnificent building. Beautiful City. Nobody looks. They miss it all – just going past.** *Joe Silvester, Pet Accessories*

And always the pigeons. They wait patiently on the railing by the War Memorial. Every so often they are startled into flight, soaring and wheeling over the market in an orchestrated frenzy, settling finally on the stone-pillared portico of City Hall to get a wider, safer view. Starlings join the pecking at dusk.

**When I was a kid I liked getting close to the birds – the starlings and pigeons.** *Sandra Pond*

Once inside the market you enter a different world, strangely disorientating and, some might say, claustrophobic: it is in the narrowness of the aisles, the lowness of the corrugated-plastic roofing, the honeycomb paving slabs.

**I love these hexagonal blocks on the floor. Like a honeycomb. I'd love to see them scrubbed a bit more though. They'd come up lovely. They're a nice size, not slippery. I love the market. I can never remember where I go or which aisle is which but I buy most things here.** *Beryl Eglington*

**It's a pain if you're tall. I have to keep my head down all the time.** *Ivan Bates*

Also, it is on a famously disorientating, vertiginous slope.

**The slope? I only ever walk up and down. I can't walk across.** *Kevin Greene, Market Manager*

**I always feel pissed when I get in there. I have to hold on to something. If I had anything to do with it, I'd get a bulldozer and make it flat. Level it. What I do like about the market is that it's like a maze. You're never quite sure where you are. It's quite nice being lost because you know you're going to get out.** *Geoffrey Patterson*

**I get that Titanic feeling ...** *Chrissie Church*

**I went to the market to buy some fabric. I felt so ill and kind of seasick and disorientated. I had to sit down on the steps of a stall with my head in my hands. What with the slope, the tilting of the awnings, and the angle of the ground, it can make you feel very wobbly.** *Kay Ohsten*

**It's very difficult standing on a hill all day. I lean when I go home. One bloke has grown one leg longer than the other just to stand up straight.** *Neil Hume, City Scenters*

**It's not good enough for people to be watching their cup of tea sliding downhill.** *T. Warburton*

At least one of the traders sees the slope as a positive asset:

> **Some people say the place makes them dizzy. Dizzy! An advertising company would die for a slogan like that – 'Norwich Market makes you DIZZY! Come for a spin.'** *Joe Silvester, Pet Accessories*

Perhaps connected with the slope, I came across a real curiosity – a study of the pelvic slouch or, to call it by its proper name, the postural function of the iliotibial tract – carried out on Norwich Market by Philip Evans, a teacher of anatomy at the Norfolk and Norwich Hospital in 1979. He came to the interesting conclusion that the iliotibial tract is the ligament that enables us to rest while standing: the ligament of idleness and boredom.

Venturing inside is to be swallowed by another world, complex, intricate, and to some people slightly threatening. To stay there for any length of time, absorbing the sights, smells, sounds, is to enter a different mental state. It is labyrinthine, full of echoes, tensions, ghosts.

> **Have you read Ursula Priestley's book on the Great Market? There's a map in there that shows the medieval market. Herbs and Spices were in just the same spot then. It made the hairs on my neck stand on end when I saw that. Continuum!** *Gareth Butcher, Herbs and Spices*

What exists there today has cascaded down the centuries from the time of the Norman Conquest. To everyone who goes there, not just to shop, but to experience, it presents a different vision: in the impulse to find metaphors and similes we can see how it touches the imagination.

**The market is a book. The stalls are the illustrations. You have to read your way through the labels. It's a massive cobweb, the spiders all working together.** *Polly Dunbar*

**It's a poem. A grid of words on a page.** *Ira Lightman*

**I love Norwich market. It's a great big vessel, an ark (which is in the word market), brimming over with all manner of busy human creatures. All the arteries of the city centre lead to the sloping stage decks of this great irksome vessel with its labyrinth of secret wings, tilting coloured canvas sails, hidden doors and portholes, crooked chimneys and shaky wood cabins. That's what it is: the hub, the engine in the centre of Norwich. I always feel seasick when I go there.** *Lys Flowerday*

**You find yourself in the middle of a film, a fair, a carousel, a fairy-tale. Something from the Middle Ages.** *Gilles Bourlet*

One trader sees the intrinsic creativity of the place.

**We're artists. Setting the stall out we create a picture every morning. It opens and shuts like a great big orchid. Every day anew. Here at the front it's important, like the cover of a book. And there's all the different seasons ... strawberry time ... daffodils.** *Joe Silvester, Pet Accessories*

The market holds a fascination for artists and photographers. Colin Self, a well-known Norfolk artist, used part of the market to furnish his own imagination in a celebrated piece made with corrugated cardboard called THE PLOUGHMAN. 'I made that with an old cauliflower box I found at the end of the day,' he said. Another artist described it as a 'barrier reef, playing host to strange mythological forms of life'.

The market opens early. First stirrings are around five o'clock with deliveries. By seven, many of the food stalls are serving their substantial breakfasts. Here you might spy a throng of fluorescent City Care

Workers refreshing themselves after work, or a swarm of green traffic wardens warming up before. I asked one of the food-stall owners what time was their busiest. 'All day,' was the answer. This is true of most of them.

Around 4 p.m. the stalls begin to close. Produce is sold off cheaply. Locking up begins.

**I love walking round when they're shutting up. So much work. So many padlocks.** *Beryl Eglington*

Barrie from the Hoover Stall is usually last to leave. One evening I returned to the market at 6.30 when the stalls were all closed. But not Barrie's. There he is, pulling things out, putting them back.

'What are you doing?' I ask.

'Looking to see what I've got.'

But eventually the voices do fall silent. The moon looks down. Then you can see the bolts and bars of the wooden cabins, the straight rows, the graffiti daubs on the red, green, yellow, and blue shutters. The empty gulleys, the pecking pigeons. The silence and darkness endow the place with a slightly sinister aspect, suggesting secrets and shadows, shady dealings, and illicit goings-on.

### ALL PROBLEMS CONCERNING THE MAINTENANCE OF THE MARKET MUST BE REPORTED TO THE MARKET OFFICE FIRST. OTHERWISE IT WILL NOT BE ATTENDED TO. THANK YOU.

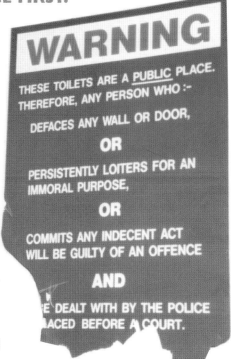

And this other-worldly underworld has its own underworld. The lavatories with their stern notices against committing a public nuisance, steel toilet bowls to protect against vandalism, their mixture of Victorian and modern tiles, their oddly municipal odour to match their stern municipal notices: 'I won't use the market lavatories,' said one trader. 'I use City Hall instead.'

Beneath the Memorial Gardens are underground lock-ups, a dark cavern where things are stored behind padlocked cages reinforced with galvanised wire. The strip-lights do little to dispel the menacing gloom of the place or to soften the tone of the notice:

I was told by more than one trader that beneath the market is another, underground market, and underground Victorian toilets 'with glass cisterns'.

**I don't know about underground tunnels, but I've heard that there are passageways between the Castle, the Guildhall and the Cathedral.** *Kevin Greene, Market Manager*

So what is so special about the place? Different things to different people:

It's like a loom. Norwich used to be at the centre of the weaving trade. Everything radiates from the market. It's a microcosm of the whole city. *Lys Flowerday*

I love everything – breakfast on the stalls – bacon butties. I take my friends from London there. My friend Fernando. They can't believe it. They hate it! Oh, but I love it. The pigeons on the striped awnings. The steaming tea. The grey drizzle. The things you can buy there. The food is local. You know where it's come from. Local radishes. Big fat leafy bunches all shiny and red. And the Eggman. All grown in Norfolk. I like the butchers too. Meat that's by Norfolk, for Norfolk, in Norfolk. Everything that Tesco's isn't. I fill up my two shopping bags and the newspaper lady tucks my *Telegraph* under my arm. I love the flowers, the fish, the spices. The traders there are very independent and hard working. I love watching the people – red-veined cheeks, tweed caps, Norfolk accents, warts. You don't see many in designer wear. I'm a romantic. It reminds me of the past. It's not anaesthetised. It's not germ-free. At eight in the morning the old boys are there, laughing, joking, bantering. It's like an island of real life. *Mark Oxley*

## A Feeling for the Place

What I love about a spud is its handshake
What I hate about tea is the takeaway cup
What I love about an orange is its slick use of language
What I hate about pine is its thirst
What I love about rain are the points that it makes
What I hate about plastic is the way that it clings
What I love about a starling is its guttersnipe sheen
What I hate about beef is its mystery
What I love about fish are the colours that are gone
What I hate about mange-tout is their appetite for travel

What I love about plastic is its eagerness to please
What I hate about a letter is knowing I may lose it
What I love about coins is the moment when they drop
What I hate about a palm is its fist
What I love about a grid is equality of space
What I hate about words is the stink when they roost
What I love about talk is its wings
What I hate about starlings are their idiotic schemes
What I love about this slope is its general inclination

*Lawrence Bradby*

'Norwich market? It's so chunky and crap. That's why it's so brilliant.'

Looking through the newspaper archives about Norwich Market, it is clear that there have always been attempts by the authorities to impose order, and an anarchic, individualistic tendency towards disorder.

> The market is anarchic. It's been there for so long. In Anglo-Saxon times it was in Tombland. Then the Normans came along and built their great big castle and moved the market to its present site. And now you've got the Town Hall and the Guildhall and Peter Mancroft. This disorderly place is surrounded on all sides by the forces of law and order. They used to hang people there. They used to burn witches and stage freak shows. And that's all still there, in a way. The market is still the riff-raff, the rebellious rabble, the governed against the governors. It's still the Anglo-Saxons versus the Normans. *Magdalen Russell*

If for 'Normans' we read City Council, and for 'Anglo-Saxons' we read Traders, we can see the antagonisms which persist to this day in their historical context – which makes it a lot more fun.

What are the other bones of contention? Mainly rents, hygiene, maintenance and regulation: but beneath these issues is a deeper tension, between the overlords and the underlings, the rulers and the ruled – and, England being England, between the different mental attitudes of our multi-layered social classes.

> The market is crowded, fizzing, a mess. That's how a market should be. The planners, Quangos, The City Centre Management Partnership – want flow. People in. People out. They look down on us from their neo-fascist building – that's what it is – have you seen the eagle winged guardians on the side of it? They want to run us down and present us with a *fait accompli*. They would turn this into Heathrow Airport Terminal One if they could. A synthetic environment. This animosity between the Traders and the City Council goes back a thousand years. Think of it. A thousand-year-old grudge. *Gareth Butcher, Herbs and Spices*

> I don't bother about the council. What's the point? You go up there in those offices and ask a question. You only get a daft answer. *James Gowing, Mike's Haberdashery*

*The Council? What do they know about the real world? They get wages.* Arthur Hunt, Casual Wear

*There's an ongoing battle with 'amenities'. They'd like to clear us off here so they can have it for functions.* David Ridgeway, Bags and Belts on the Haymarket

*The council? We call them the Kremlin. I leave 'em alone. They like to be on a pedestal. We used to have a raffle to fund a pool for prizes. But then we had to use the funds to fight the council's rent rises.* Lenny Nixon, Army Surplus

*The council keeps complaining. They want us to draw back. They don't like us spilling into the aisles. They'd like 30 per cent of our takings.* Jimmy Cossey, Electrical

Some of the traders are of the firm belief that the Council is deliberately running the market down in order to get rid of it altogether. A common complaint is that little of the money the council collects in rent from the stall-holders goes towards its maintenance.

*I'd like to know what happens to the rent I pay every month.* Anita Pickering, Butcher

*We like our market as it is. If the council had cleaned the tilts and cleaned out the gutters once in a while, they wouldn't be in the state they're in now. But they won't clean them. You know the reason they give? Environmental Health.* Miriam Bowgen, Cary's Flowers

*It's grubby, dirty, downtrodden. You'd get more interest from people if they [the council] scrubbed the floor once a week and gave the whole place a lick of paint. That wouldn't spoil the atmosphere. People won't shop on a market if it's not clean. You can only neglect a place for so long before it falls down.* Anita Pickering, Butcher

Others put their faith in the knowledge that in 1341 Edward III, much pleased with the people of Norwich, granted the franchise of the market to the city's rulers 'in perpetuity'.

*They can't close down the market. We've got a royal charter from the king. It used to be run by the Church of Peter Mancroft. Now it's the City Council. Some people call the councillors pigs but I think the Council is very good. So is the Market Manager. But you can't regiment a market. You've got to keep a market a market. The traders are very insecure. You're only as good as your last week. So we like a bit of a fight. We like to think they're up to something. We're like kids in a playground. When the headmaster's away, we play.* Joe Silvester, Pet Accessories

*It's our market, not the council's. It belongs to the people of Norwich.* Roy Macleish, Events cards stall

Kevin Greene, the Market Manager, is the go-between:

**There's this problem with 'encroachment'. The traders at the front push the boundaries further and further forward. The traders at the back follow suit and block the aisles. The traders in the middle object because they are paying the same money for less. We have to work really hard to get them all to stay within bounds. It's not something we like doing. No sooner have we done so than a city councillor tells them it's quite all right to spread themselves out. No wonder the traders think we don't know what we're up to.**

**I see my job as keeping a balance between the council and the traders – piggy in the middle. It's a thankless task in a way. Nobody ever tells me I'm doing a good job.**

Another source of dispute is Health and Hygiene. It wasn't so long ago that Edgar Oddey used to sell horse-meat fresh from the Yarmouth track. He would chop the carcasses on the stall for dog meat so that the blood ran straight off the stall and on to the floor. The gully ran with blood. Every so often he would swill it with a bucket of water. What would Health and Safety say to that now?

Then there is a chip corner where people take shelter while they eat, usually next to an overflowing rubbish bin. But the bin serves a purpose. It's where people put the chip bags when they've finished.

There is nothing new in these issues. In 1967 a public-health inspector called Mr Horne declared that the market was 'unfit for any unwrapped food, except fruit, vegetables and eggs'. In 1982, at the other extreme, the Traders Chairman was stunned at the decision of the council to install wash-basins and sinks. 'This really is going too far,' he said.

Weights and measures – overcharging for less than the required quantity – is not such a problem now as it used to be. It's no longer possible to get away with selling 'over-priced beer in undersized pottes' as William Collard did in 1564, but conversion from imperial to metric, on 1st January 2001 caused general confusion and suspicion. Despite customer resisitance, the traders where obliged to enforce it.

**I write all my own labels. I like writing. It took me three days to re-label all these for January 1st when we went metric. But you have to. It's the law. *Gareth Butcher, Herbs and Spices***

There is tension between the increasing tendency to regulate, and the desire to keep the shabbiness of the market, which is seen as part of its character; between change, and resistance to change; a sentimental attachment to the old and a desire for the new.

**Nobody wants change. But change has to come. I remember before they paved Gentlemen's Walk. There was uproar. They said it would drive trade away if people can't park their cars. But who wants the cars back now? *Joe Silvester, Pet Accessories***

**Norwich market? It's so chunky and crap. That's why it's so brilliant.** *Rebecca Atkinson*

'Most Norwich people love their market with its gay, coloured tilts and teeming life,' wrote a citizen in 1957, while a visitor expressed her disgust with the place by saying that she 'couldn't help comparing Norwich to a rosy red apple with a rotting core'.

The debate continues today, fear that the atmosphere will be lost against the need for change. In 1968 Jack Edwards, an EDP correspondent, called it 'an urban masterpiece, a work of art, the best example of town planning in the country today'. While in 1942 the Whiffler described the terraced gardens round the War Memorial as 'a wonderful sight, the best window box in the country'. No one can deny today that this same scene looks decidedly dog-eared. One brave councillor made some suggestions:

> **I went to Barcelona with my wife Delia. The market there is magnificent, the displays fantastic. On my return I suggested at a committee meeting that the market-traders should be trained in the art of display. Next thing I knew there was a cartoon of me in the paper as a stuffed pig with an apple in my mouth!** *Andy Permain, City Councillor*

> **They're talking about changing the market. Sterilising it. Health and safetying it to death.** *Hugh Ferrier*

> **Modernise? They want me to 'ave a plate-glass window. I expect I'll end up serving me cockles through an 'atch on the end of a stick.** *Cockle stall-holder*

> **Well, if you're asking me if I wouldn't rather be in a nice warm centrally-heated office drinking coffee with beautiful women walking around instead of in this open, tawdry, atmosphere, thinking 'Will she, won't she, buy something?' The answer is: yes, I would.** *Jimmy Cossey, Electrical*

> **I've been here eight years. The market is crap. Scruffy. They should knock it down and start again.** *Tim Futter, Candle Stall*

> **They shouldn't change the market. They did it up in the seventies but now it's lovely and old and tatty again.** *Sandra Pond*

The shabbiness is not only an essential part of the ambience of the market, but also provokes a certain ambivalence in its customers. Even in a city as unusually egalitarian as Norwich, snobbery and the class system prevail.

> **I have chips for lunch – or mushy peas – but only if I'm with someone I know well.** *Hugh Ferrier*

> **I've been coming to the market since my school-days in 1972. I like mushy peas, bacon sandwiches**

dripping in fat, chips. A lot of people won't come here any more though. It's snobbery. The middle classes don't want to be seen here. I took an American friend from California to the mushy-pea stall.

'Do you have anything like this in America?' I asked.

'No, thank Gawd!' he said.

He thought it was the tip of the third world. *Will Giles*

Even smart business people from Norwich Union and places come here. They like to get away from their offices. *Beryl Warner*

My sister's a teacher and she's married to a city councillor. She wouldn't be seen dead on the market. *Eileen*

Some people take offence at things. 'Don't you darling me!' they say. Or they say, 'I won't buy one of them. I'll go to a proper shop.' *Joe Silvester, Pet Accessories*

I come from Sprowston on my moped. I don't know what my friends would say if they saw me here. *Veronica Clark*

## "Ere, come on lady, this aint Sainsbury's yer know!'

I don't go to supermarkets. I like a proper grapefruit. *Beryl Eglington*

I buy meat on the market. There are a couple of traditional butchers here. I can't bear that supermarket meat, all pink and damp in all that plastic packaging. *Veronica Clark*

The supermarkets have had a profound effect on shopping habits. What we gain in choice, ease, convenience, we lose in experience. Something in our hunter/gatherer instinct is thwarted, so that shopping is for many a tedious chore rather than a satisfying achievement. We fill up our trolleys, put the bags in the car boot, and then have the equally tiresome chore of putting it all away. Then we feel guilty for finding it tiresome. We are spoilt for choice when much of the world goes hungry.

To shop on the market is quite different: it often means comparing the products on the different stalls, and the purchase is accompanied by a human exchange – a joke, advice, or the occasional argument. It is all less predictable and more time consuming. It is not for people in a hurry.

We are seduced in ever greater numbers by the supermarkets – open all hours; freedom of choice; priority to customer demands – and perhaps only unconsciously do we feel the erosion of human intimacy on which our sense of well-being depends.

It changes so fast, people don't seem to last. It's all because of the supermarkets. *Archie Stagg*

The biggest effect has been the reduction in the number of stalls selling fruit and vegetables.

I've been on the market 25 years. I used to sell fruit and vegetables but there were too many of us. In those days we would start at five in the morning and be sold out by two. *Joe Silvester, Pet Accessories*

But are the effects entirely negative? A common complaint was that some of the traders would have a fine display of produce at the front and serve inferior stuff from the back. But supermarket customers are groomed in the art of making their own choices – a practice which some traders tried in vain to discourage.

**You couldn't touch the fruit in those days. Everyone would have gone mad. You either want it or you don't. But times change. You've got to keep ahead.** *Joe Silvester, Pet Accessories*

A letter to the EDP in 1967 complains thus: 'My wife asked one stall-holder if she might be allowed to point out the tomatoes she wanted. The man launched into violent and disgusting abuse at this – nearby stall-holders abetting him. My wife ran from the market extremely alarmed. When I saw her later she was in an extremely nervous condition.'

Another letter in 1970 says: 'on two separate occasions last month I witnessed a youth in one of the fruit and vegetable stalls making rude and provoking noises with his mouth at visitors to the market who were visibly annoyed'.

**When I was between 6 and 12 in the 1940s, I well remember shopping trips to the market with my mother, where she used to buy all her fruit, vegetables and fish. She was rather wary of the stall-holders and used to say they arranged all the best stuff in pyramids on the front of the stall and serve you with inferior stuff from the back. Many a time she would march back accusing the man of 'fobbing her off' with a rotten cauliflower or smelly fish. In those days stall-holders really didn't like you to choose your own, or to say that cabbage please. You had to take what you were given. Only quite recently I was choosing a couple of oranges and the trader said, "Ere, come on lady, this aint Sainsbury's yer know!'** *Kay Ohsten*

So the supermarkets in that sense have been an influence for the better! And on the food stalls, tea is no longer served in cracked cups.

But every town, every village, every settlement, began with a market, with this old system of human exchange of goods for money: how long will this last in the face of all the encouragement to shop online?

I see the market as the last bastion of this old system of bartering. It's also all that stands between me and my fear of the internet. I do buy things on the internet – it's the only way some young designers can operate. But the market is the place for real human interaction. It's where you talk to people. And listen. I like to hear the old boys talk over the newspaper headlines in the morning. They make me smile inside. *Philip Browne*

The market industry is one of the biggest chain stores there is. Two hundred and sixty thousand people work in it. They offer a personal service and a different slant. They symbolise freedom of choice, free enterprise, the age-old free exchange of goods for money. They are the only things that keep the supermarket monster at bay. But, of course, the supermarkets offer uniformity and perfectly formed fruit. *Kevin Greene, Market Manager*

The irony is, of course, that the more we relinquish to the supermarkets, the more they consolidate, the narrower our choice.

**'Norwich Market is as ugly and dangerous and dark as it's generous and kind.'**

**There's a lot of dark stuff going on. Under-the-counter stuff. I'd like to know more about the dark stuff.** *Magdalen Russell*

The market was at one time a much more brutal place than it is now. There were hangings and floggings and freak shows. Ears were cut off and witches put to death. The most common misdemeanors, then as now, were drunkenness, brawling, swearing, fornication, thieving. Only the punishments were more severe, more publicly enjoyed. In the court records we can see this element of entertainment. In March 1578 there is a reference to Swayne's wife who stole a goose and roasted it. She was 'set in the stocks with a goose around her neck'. In December 1622 William Chapman, 'for selling mustie oatemeal', was dealt the same punishment, 'with half a peck of mustie meal by him'.

There are more unusual offences: in 1551 William Collerd, a cobbler by trade, was challenged by Alderman Davy, one of the ruling élite, for defying the authorities by 'wearing a beard'.

The lack of public toilets was a problem. In August 1621 a labourer called James Lowe was set in the stocks 'for burying a necessary in the castle dykes'.

More gruesomely, in 1660 an unfortunate musician called William Mason was 'set upon the pillory and his ears nailed to the same for the devising of unfitting songs'.

Quite often the victims were released from the pillory by having their ears 'cropped' – in other words, chopped off. Whipping 'at post' or 'about the market with papers on ther hede' was the common punishment for whoredom and fornication.

Something lingers of this history. At night the graffiti-sprawled shutters, the padlocks, the long aisles and low roofs, in the all-pervading gloom, the market looks positively sinister, an appropriate setting for murder and mayhem, secrets, and skulduggery.

**The market is as ugly and dangerous and dark as it's wonderful and generous and kind.** *Magdalen Russell*

So I went looking for the dark stuff.

**You want to know about the dark side of the market? We're not going to tell you are we? But if you want the dark side – look at the city council. Look at Management. Look at the American Administration. That's where you'll find the dark side. One of the management – in the past – not now – whose name I won't mention, was as bent as two horseshoes standing on end. He had more twists than the great wall of china. He even looked like a mafia godfather. Yes, there is a bit of corruption amongst the traders, but it's innocent corruption.** *Gareth Butcher, Herbs and Spices*

The most sensational item I unearthed in recent years was the misbehaviour of Joe Silvester's parrot, Dickie, in 1983. Dickie took up his perch at Joe's pet stall with a few choice words and a 'passable imitation of an ambulance siren'. There were many complaints and Dickie was dispatched to an out-of-town pet shop. There was also the tall stranger who appeared early one morning in 1958 and bought £500 worth of fruit and vegetables, and then disappeared 'to fetch his van' without paying. At the end of the day the stall-holders found themselves with a mountain of unsold produce. There were black-outs and shortages during the war and power cuts in the seventies. I looked for shady practices and blackguardly deeds, but the worst piece of recorded villainy was a stall-holder prosecuted for selling fake designer-labels.

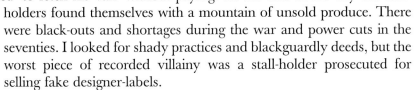

There is drug dealing, of course, but not on the market itself, rather on the perimeters. Pornography has found much more profitable hunting ground on the internet. To this observer it seems that the traders work too hard in adverse conditions to have the mindset for serious skulduggery.

**One little fella with ginger hair got chucked out for selling tobacco.** *Norman Rush*

**There's a lot going on here. You just have to watch. Furtive, under the counter, people hiding from each other. You watch who goes where. Not drugs, no. Contraband! Whisky. Cigarettes!**

**I love the market, it's the biggest thing Norwich has got. I love the freshness, the bubble, the atmosphere, the people. I don't love the burglaries though. We've had five in the last week. The burglars can get in everywhere. They even run along the roofs.** *Stella Arthurton, Harry's Tea Stall*

**I do get occasional shoplifters. I caught two once. I was a bit upset because they were regular customers. I just took the bag back. But whenever they went past the stall after that they shouted 'Rubbish bags'. I just pretended not to hear them.**

Another time someone stole a whole ring of bags. I caught up with them in the taxi-stand. They were selling them on for £5 each I'm not brave but I just took them back. Whoever did it was spaced out. They just don't seem to realise that you've worked hard for what you've got. But you've got to trust people. On the whole, people are very nice. *Jane Spanton, Bags Plus*

Tracy [her assistant interrupts] 'No they're not. They're very rude. They don't say 'please' and 'thank you'.

You do get shoplifters. You'd be surprised at the types. Middle-aged ladies. Respectable looking. We stop them and ask them to pay double for the goods or we'll call the police. And we don't give them the goods. The police aren't interested. They wouldn't do anything anyway. *Anon.*

Yes, there's contraband on the market. Only tobacco. You can make £400 for £40 worth of cigarettes. The police keep a close eye. They caught the market Santa Klaus one year. Just before Christmas. They filmed him delivering in the van. So Father Christmas was arrested. No alcohol or drugs though. *Harold Jeffrey*

There is a bit of contraband – mainly tobacco – but that's a problem for Customs and Excise. Civil law, not criminal. There used to be some really tough people ruled the market and regular fisticuffs. Not now. *Kevin Greene, Market Manager*

What corruption there is, isn't always the province of the traders.

We still have to work hard to dispel the trader's distrust from past practices – backhanders – brown envelopes – that sort of thing. *Kevin Greene, Market Manager*

So, despite vague mutterings that this man was a murderer, that man a dealer in stolen goods, my search for the dark stuff ended in disappointment. 'Talk to Florrie,' I'd been told. 'She's full of scurrilous tales.' But I never did find Florrie. The only shockingly cruel thing I heard was that some of the traders locked an unfortunate paraplegic into a huge cardboard carton and left him hollering for hours in the underground lock-ups.

**'The wind was blowing on Monday and the rain was raining, but we were still here.'**

The weather and the changing seasons is part of the raw, elemental quality of the market, that which keeps us in touch with our human selves. People look around the stalls comparing produce and prices. They dodge

wind and rain in the gaps between the stalls: wet–dry–wet–dry. Patchwork weather. They choose their fish (and some mighty strange ones at that) and have them gutted, beheaded and wrapped in proper paper. Though the seasons are shifting inexorably – you can buy tulips and daffodils on the market at Christmas – the fresh produce on the whole is seasonal. Strawberries, raspberries, red-currants, blackberries, are piled high in the summer and sold off cheaply around four o'clock. There is purple-sprouting broccoli in spring; tasty celery with real dirt in the autumn and earthy leeks. There are pumpkins and squashes at Hallowe'en. It is also a whole lot cheaper than the shops.

**In winter the smell of fresh celery was marvellous. The stall-holders had a galvanised bath full of water and scrubbed the black 'fen' soil off the celery. Not allowed today. But that celery had taste.**
*Barry Guymer*

Even on the wettest, greyest, most miserable day, there are radios, light, food, friendship, objects strange and varied, smells, sounds, bustle, warmth, contact. Something in the energy and intimacy of all this generates its own kind of heat.

Its hard. But it's no harder than digging a hole in the road. We're here in all weathers. The wind was blowing on Monday and the rain was raining, but we were still here. 'Playdays' we call them, because there aren't many customers. *Joe Silvester, Pet Accessories*

We have a slow period from January to March. We call that the 'kipper' season. *Arthur Hunt, Casual Wear*

You get used to the weather. We don't get cold days no more. Not like we used to. *Paddy*

On a cold, gloomy, rainy Saturday I drag myself into the market to soak up what I expect will be a gloomy atmosphere. The first chill of winter. There is much rubbing of hands and stamping of feet. Flat drizzles of hair. People trying to dodge the squares of rain from the gaps in the roof. A pigeon shivers on top of a flag-pole.

**You have to wear lots of layers in the winter.** *Jane Spanton, Bags Plus*

Some days are freezing. Despite the layers of vests, tights, socks, my legs are so cold they're nearly dropping off. Mushy peas and cups of tea don't reach. Polly paints a fireplace on my story-stall together with a large friendly ginger moggy. Strange. I feel warmer. I have lights, candles, mistletoe.

**Look at my hands. All split. Chapped hands. Chapped lips. Chapped feet. I go home and I go to sleep. It's all this coming in and out of the cold.** *Alex Pond*

But the constant exposure appears to have no ill effect.

**No, I don't feel the cold. And no, I never take a day off. Only if I've got to go to the doctor or the dentist.** *Mrs M. Reid, Slipper Stall*

**I'm never ill. Never had a day off. All the fresh air! You can't ring in sick with a job like this.** *Richard Anderson, Menswear*

**No, I've never had a day off. Being in the fresh air means you never get ill.** *John Kett, Roots and Fruits*

**I come here all through the day, usually with my little shopper. This morning there were beautiful snowflakes. A hard frost and sunshine. There's a good balance of enclosed and open here. I'd like to come early in the morning when they're bringing stuff in. But I never do. Maybe I will when the weather's better.** *Beryl Eglington*

**I'm an outdoor girl. You prepare for it – wrap up in your thermals and your long johns.** *Paula Taylor, Cheese stall*

On a freezing cold day, Radio Norfolk blares from the ice-cream stall, which is decorated with flags. 'How do you sell ice-cream in this weather?' I ask.

'Believe it or not, we sell a lot. I get up at six in the morning, and I'm up and running by 7.45. Every day,' says Theresa Wright.

Knowledge is Bought in the Market

You say, and stride the tilted, drunken rows.
These Norwich cries and bawls have thronged the air
for years between St Peter Mancroft and
the Guildhall. Farmers' red-cheeked wives sat there
on cobbles. Cabbages and eggs in peds,
those half-moon baskets, set in front of them.
Then windburned men sold eastern silks like flames,
Low Country pots, old charms, fresh bread and gems,
lace, salted herrings, olive oil from Spain,
gold trinkets, chickens, harnesses and reins.

As always, city/country meet in scents:
the wholesome balm of local carrot fields
mixed well with fragrant foreign spices, reeks
of blighted produce artfully concealed.
You taste iced pastries, savour cheese, know where
pale lemon soles and cockles may be found.
In summer: cherries, apricots and plums.
In winter: glowing tangerines in mounds.
You touch soft muslins, test new boots and jeans.
See stalls as theatres with changing scenes.

You hear that there's a writer's booth up there
with words to choose, and questions, answers too.
She piles up words like sweets. You test them, speak
and write, and learn some things you never knew.

*Jenny Morris*

**'You can eat like a King here. From roast pork to mushy peas.'**

I make my way through the outdoor market. As you turn up the middle you get layers of smells. You can almost eat them: cheeses, pies, bread, coffee, and there's a certain spot where it all mingles together. But the best is the crisp, hot-fat smell of chips that's getting to me right this minute.
(From *The Spying Game*, by Pat Moon)

Clustered haphazardly between rows B and E are the food stalls: HARRY'S PLACE, REGGIE'S, RUBY'S TEAS, BRENDA'S TEA STALL, MUSHY PEAS, JANE'S CATERING, HENRY'S HOG-ROAST AND CARVERY, LUCY'S TRADITIONAL CHIPS, KEY'S CHIP'N DIP, FISH AND CHIPS. More recently, CHINA WOK. The names set the tone: friendly, personal, intimate.

**When I'm away from the market I think of stripes and squares. When I'm here it's honeycomb. I always come in between Tools and Flowers and I think Food! Food! Food! I'm a male!** *Duncan*

It is such a close-knit jigsaw that if you buy a cup of tea on one stall and look around, there is a real chance that you'll put your empty cup down on another. I imagine the stalls know their own cups and that they usually find their way home. 'Sugar, darling?' they say, if you ask for a cup of tea, spoon at the ready.

To counteract the slope of the ground, many of the counters have been built to slope upwards. The idea was to even things out to produce a level surface. Instead, the ground slopes down, the counter careers up, so that your eyes have some trouble in adjusting to the wedge shape in-between. You lose all sense of normal perspective. The sink on the mushy-pea stall is straight out of hickory-dickory land.

**Have you noticed the sink on the mushy-pea stall? It's slanty. Makes you feel drunk.** *Sandra Pond*

The worse the weather, the busier these stalls. The steaming and the smelling, the sizzling and the frying, the bubbling and the boiling begins with the break of day. By 7 a.m. there are throngs of people round all the food stalls. On the greyest, gloomiest, dreariest of days it can all be as festive as a picnic.

The food is traditional, stomach-warming, filling, tasty, cheap: bacon and eggs; fish and chips; bacon rolls; sandwiches of all kinds; the infamous mushy peas with pepper and mint sauce; steaming hot mugs of tea; oxtail soup and onions. The atmosphere is like the old-style transport cafés so beloved of lorry drivers. There

is none of the ceremonious pretentiousness of Little Chef and other places, and if the food can sometimes be classed as high-cholesterol junk, it is a lot more tempting and varied than the high-street burger.

Rickety tin chimneys with cowls break through the canopies, every so often burping out a puff of smoke. They provide the perfect perch for the seagulls, pigeons, starlings, ready to snatch the scraps.

**As a kid my mum used to drag me around looking for the cheapest carrots. I would get fed up. It always seemed to be raining. I was too thin. My Mum would force me to eat a bacon sandwich.** *Sandra Pond*

**We came to find the source of the smoke we've seen rising above the stalls.** *Laura Fish and son Joshua*

All kinds of people come here: poor, middling, rich, business people, professionals, workers from local building sites (at the time of writing those working on the new Millennium Library), street performers, Big Issue sellers, people in wheelchairs, lost souls, lunatics, poets, lovers. Some come to talk, some to look, some to stare at the counter, some to read their newspapers. The only people who don't come here are those who have an aversion to Brobdingnagian close-ups of strange complexions or an air-freshener mentality. It's almost impossible if you go here on a regular basis not to strike up a conversation with a stranger. 'Enjoyin' that?' they might ask. Or, 'Pass the mint sauce, darling?'

More devastatingly, someone might say, 'Two years ago today my wife died.'

**I come here every morning for a cup of tea before I start work. Not just a cup of tea. I like people-watching. I like listening. You meet all sorts of people.** *Beryl Warner*

**We come here every day for breakfast. Dinner too. You get a proper dinner for £1.75.**
*Crumpled couple*

**I was waiting at Brenda's tea stall for ages. All I wanted was a cup of tea. But the girl didn't serve me. All she wanted was to scrub the place clean. I got one in the end though.** *Maggie*

Some people come for their staple meal of the day. Ninety pence will buy egg on toast and a cup of tea or a bowl of mushy peas. Mandy's Tea Stall advertises a BELLYBUSTER. This includes bacon, eggs, sausages, tomatoes, mushrooms, beans and toast. All for £3. You can have the even bigger BELLYBREAKER: three bacon, two eggs, two sausages, sauté potatoes, mushrooms, beans, fried slice, toast.

'Do people actually eat all that?' I ask.

'They do. Sometimes they come back for another lot at eleven.'

**I like it here. Nice food. Lots of laughs. More real than your up-market caff. Better than watching crap T.V.** *Paul*

Pinned up at Sue's Snack Stall is a poster:

**Fifteen reasons why a dog is better than a man:**
**Middle-aged dogs don't feel the need to drop you for a younger owner.**
**Dogs don't feel guilt ...**

A man looks over my shoulder as I read it.

'I hope you don't agree with that,' he says.

'Do you?' I ask.

He reads it slowly. 'Yes I do,' he says.

'So should I get myself a dog?'

'No,' he says, 'get a cat.'

**Every day I order lunch from Sue's stall. There's something different every day. Today it was cheese and potato pie. I just phone in and say, 'What's for lunch, Sue?'** *Colin Stephenson, Natural Medicines*

I have childhood memories of Norwich market. I discovered the mushy-peas stall in my early teens. I thought it was great. Green, tasty, with mint sauce and pepper! And a white roll to mop it all up. I quickly introduced my whole family to it. They loved it too. I left Norwich several years ago but still like wandering though the market sniffing in the smells of the food stalls! *Geraint Powell*

### PUT BRITISH PORK ON YOUR FORK
**HOT PORK ROAST WITH CRACKLING, APPLE SAUCE, ONIONS**
**£2**
**HOT BEEF ROAST WITH MUSTARD AND HORSE RADISH**
**£2.10**
**THICK SLICES IN A BAP £2.20**

You can eat like a King here. From roast pork to mushy peas. *Ros Newman*

I'm from Lowestoft. I've worked here for four years. It's very boring in January, February, March. But OK the rest of the time. I expect I'll stay here until the place falls down really. *Paul Smith, Henry's Hog Roast*

Mushy Peas! I have them for lunch three days a week. Especially after a hangover. Then I have a pie and peas and then another bowl of peas. *Philip Browne*

I had my first mushy peas the other day. At first I thought 'yuck!' but my stomach felt cosy all afternoon. *Susan*

I became a regular at Reggie's in 1977. A large elderly lady of great presence used to serve ham off the bone. And dripping on toast. I graduated from that to mushy peas and then to my staple: chicken rolls. But I always had a real mug of tea made with real tea leaves. And the rolls were always fresh. That's what's so good about the food stalls: it's always fresh stuff. Who wants rolls which are cold and damp? I don't. In the last couple of years Reggie's have introduced wholemeal rolls (the round buns). I don't know where they get them from, but they're very good – good texture and body, not light and fluffy.

I was lured away from Reggie's to Harry's by the bacon rolls. The smell and the sight of those lush rashers! They always give you plenty of bacon – not meagre little pieces. You always get a good helping of whatever it is on the food stalls. And you see the uncooked bacon or sausages, so you always know what you're eating. I've had hot pork rolls there in the past, too, with apple sauce. Very moreish. From bacon rolls I graduated to 'sausage in a roll' – again with plenty of sausage in a decent-sized roll, and even a couple of sausages in one roll if the sausages looked a bit small. The same high-quality mug of tea there.

My current favourite is Ruby's because the choice is healthier than the others – there's always salad in the rolls if you want it – and the mugs of tea are truly gigantic. I favour the turkey and salad rolls, but also like the ham and the pork. The stall is personal because Ruby herself always serves you and remembers that you are a regular. She is very calm, sweet and motherly. All the food is marvellously fresh, and you can always have your own peculiar tastes catered for – although I'm a mainliner. It's very, very clean.

I don't really take much notice of the people around me when I'm eating there. All sorts really, including layabouts and down-and-outs sometimes. Everyone is treated with respect and kindness. There was a bloke, years ago, who used to appear at Reggie's wearing full red-coated hunting gear – black riding hat, white jodhpurs, riding boots, and carrying a riding crop. He had a loud upper-class voice, and God knows where he came from. His red coat was slightly faded and seedy, if I remember rightly. *Michael Cullup*

## CHIPS FROM 50p. JUMBO HOT DOGS. JUMBO BACON ROLLS.

An empty stall near the food stalls serves as the chip corner. There are always people there. People standing silently in their own spaces. An old woman with no teeth struggling to squash the chips with her gums. Next to an overflowing rubbish bin a young girl is eating chips. She has lots of face piercings, three rings on her nose, one on her eyebrows, others on her eyes. She is thin and pale except for a red raw graze on her forehead. She also has two fading black eyes. She crams the chips into her mouth, then blows. They are too hot. At the food stall nearby a big blonde woman is smoking and talking to her big blonde friend. Her small child pulls down her tights and pees into a drain. No one notices. The child looks pleased and peers down the drain.

Great chips. No cars. *Angie, aged 53*

My Mum gets annoyed because I'm always eating chips. Chips and chips again. *Brendan Johnson, aged 13*

'Ow can we be expected to keep the passages clear? Where would we eat our chips? *Brad*

43

Two men are having hot, steaming bowls of mushy peas after their lunch-time drinking session.

'Do you come here often?' I ask.

'Never!' they reply.

I like egg and bacon sandwiches from Reggie's, with sliced tomato and brown sauce. They fry it nice and greasy there. *Kevin Joyce (Griff)*

I've been coming to the market since my school-days in 1972. I like mushy peas and bacon sandwiches dripping in fat. *Will Giles*

On a cold and crispy day I like to have a bacon roll and a cup of coffee. Sometimes I have chips. I like to listen to the gossip. The market is my social life. *Veronica Clark*

Norwich would be nothing without the market. You get the best cup of tea in the world here. And a nice egg and cress roll. *Margaret*

*(William Shakespeare, Comedy of Errors, 1. 2.13)*

## 'He's like a mole with his heap and his shovel paws.'

A less homogenous bunch of people would be hard to find. Some are born and bred into market trading, others are the young and newly enterprising who use the market as a first step towards creating their own business. Some have travelling backgrounds, while several have university degrees, or some other professional or arts qualifications. What is undoubtedly true is that the market is a place where the spirit of idiosyncratic individuality is allowed to flourish without the necessity for business plans, cash flows, market strategies, and so forth.

All of the traders work hard in all weathers. Standing around in January or February when there is less trade is just as challenging to the spirit as being rushed off your feet in December. Most are in it for love of the place, or the product, or both. All like being their own boss. The stalls are worlds unto themselves, their owners often known by their produce: Leather-man, Cheeseman, Egg-man, Hoover-man, Knicker-lady, China-woman, Flower-boy.

Despite this independence, the spirit on the market is one of co-operation rather than competitiveness.

**Everyone knows one another on the market. We look out for one another. I know most of the customers and what they want.** *Paula Taylor, Cheese Stall*

**We have a great laugh at Christmas and we get lots of cards from the customers. You don't get that in supermarkets.** *Joe Silvester, Pet Accessories*

Tea arrives:

**That's from Ray in the next stall. He always sends me a mug when he has one.** *Jane Spanton, Bags Plus*

**There's no competition between the flower-sellers on the market. If one of us runs out of stuff, someone else will give it to them. It was the same when I was young. The fruit-and-veg stalls were back to back. If you noticed that someone had run out of cucumbers, you gave them yours. That's how it was. No problem.** *Paddy, flower-seller*

> **There are friendly people all around. Everyone speaks to each other. We help each other out.**
> *Joanna Furze, Lace Curtains*

The traders tend to do things in their own time and in their own way. People are always calling in on Andy 'leather-man's' stall, for a cup of tea and a chat. Quite often he's not there. At other times he has visitors: young women bring their babies; young men their jackets and trousers. No time-and-motion study here.

Many of the traders mentioned the 'characters' that used to exist in the old days. Universal education up to the age of 16, and the all-pervasive influence of the media tend to standardise people and their way of thinking. This is probably the last generation to have escaped that process. So the market is a bastion not only of free enterprise, but free-thinking, free-spiritedness, and a determination to do things their way.

## BARRIE
## THE HOOVER STALL

In the centre of the market is the strangest stall of all: Barrie's hoover stall. Like giant entrails, or an artificial brain, or the tentacles of a dismembered octopus, it squats there, a snaking, coiling, tangled, groping, mountainous muddle of hoses and bags. Barrie has everything and anything to do with vacuum cleaners. The wonder is that he can find anything.

But word has it that no matter how old your vacuum cleaner is, no matter what model, no matter how small and insignificant the missing or broken part, Barrie can find it for you.

**The hoover stall is amazing. He's got everything to do with hoovers. He has every part. My old hoover broke down and he fixed it.** *David Adlard*

Barrie is constantly tending, sorting and tidying through the piles of bags and packets and plugs and wires. Barrie is not communicative. 'Talk to you later,' he says when I approach him.

He has the intensely focused, blinkered gaze of the true obsessive. I make two or three careful approaches, always getting the same obliquely delivered response, 'Talk to you later.'

**Barrie is always first here and last to leave. It's sometimes eight o'clock by the time he's put all this stuff away. 'E likes it. 'E works for 'iself. 'E never finishes. Sometimes 'e goes to fix a washing machine or something and I look after his stall.** *Harold Jeffrey*

**Barrie's a National Resource. My mother-in-law had a kettle from the 1950s and some idiot let it boil dry and the element burnt out. I asked him if he could replace it. 'Give me a minute,' he says. He's like a mole with his heap and his shovel paws. You see his legs disappear into this coal heap at 45 degrees. A moment later he reappears with something wrapped in rust-retardant paper. An element for my mother's kettle! Another time I see a bloke walking up with his ancient vacuum cleaner. Some part of it was broken and he didn't know the model so he brought the whole thing in. But you never see Barrie smile. You work overtime to make him smile.** *Gareth Butcher, Herbs and Spices*

After several failed approaches, Barrie talks to me!

**I was going to write you a story. My father had a stall going back 30 years. Tools. Then he tried all sorts of things – cards, fishing tackle, until I fell into this. That was when I left school twenty years ago. I can supply most parts for most machines, going back to when they were first made. I do cooker parts and fridge and freezer parts as well as hoovers. I can usually find things. If I can't find it straight away I say go away and do your shopping, then come back and I'll have it for you. Nowadays people often have two hoovers – the old one that they keep upstairs, and the new one downstairs, especially some old gals who can't lift things easily.**

I close when I feel like it, but it is usually very late, long after other people have gone home. Sometimes I enjoy what I do. Sometimes I don't.

Harold comes over and talks about the terrible treatment his wife had when she was dying of lymph cancer. 'One day,' says Barrie, 'we'll wonder about the barbaric way we treat people today.' He promises to look after Harold's rings when he dies. 'I'll polish them every day.'

Barrie's stall is a truly original creation, an artistic installation. Somebody should try to Save It For The Nation.

### DAVID POINDEXTER
### O'BABY

David is in his thirties. He sells everything for babies from 0–2 years: clothes, prams, toys.

I've been open for seven weeks. We had a little one sixteen months ago. There's nowhere in the city to buy things for babies except Mothercare and Bonds. I spotted a niche in the market. There's a waiting list for stalls in the market. I've got two so that's about £5,000 I needed to start up. It's risky. You've got to be able to support yourself for six months or a year before people know you're here. I advertised – put flyers out. There's no passing trade in this aisle. I've got retail experience and my wife's an accountant so our ultimate aim is to have a shop. But I've got no illusions about making a fortune. You've got to be realistic. It's no good giving

up after a month. The other traders are very helpful. They give you general feedback. I sell branded stuff – but it's cheaper than in the shops because I've got no overheads. Twenty years ago I worked in the Arcade. The market is tatty and dirty, and that's a pity.

### JOANNA FURZE
### LACE CURTAINS
### SUPPLIERS OF LINENS,
### FURNISHING

Joanna takes a break from writing out her Christmas cards.

The stall has been here for 30 or 40 years. I've been here for six years and I work five days a week from 8.30 to 4.30. I get three weeks holiday a year. It's freer here and more relaxed than a shop. People get a more personal service. I'll help them work out the measurements, and so on. Some people say net curtains are out of fashion – but there are plenty of people who want to buy them. But I look in the windows on my drive home. I never see my nets. I can't understand it. I sell so many. I know my stock very well. The market is a bit shabby. I never shopped here before I worked here. But you can get everything you want. It's a bit slow in January and February, and that gets you down. But I never get cold.

# ROY ANDERSON
## ANDERSON'S MENSWEAR

Roy has silver-sand hair and gold-rimmed glasses. His looks belie his 71 years. His son Richard works for him. Roy plays golf at Hunstanton on Fridays and Saturdays. He sells a wide range of men's clothing (two shirts for £5, padded fleeces) and footwear, from trendy Doc Martens to traditional green wellies. He has four stalls in all.

I came on to the market when I was 15. We sold government surplus. In those days, after the war, there wasn't much around. I work here three days a week now. It used to be six. I keep saying I don't want to come, but I come anyway.

The market's changed a lot. All the characters – they've gone now. They used to 'pitch' in the old days, stand and shout their wares – crockery, cutlery, things like that. A big crowd would gather round. That stopped in the sixties. And down this side it was all chickens. There were 100 fruit-and-vegetable stalls. You could buy corn cures and things to stop your glasses steaming up. There were plenty of laughs.

The world comes to you in a market-place. I've seen lots of famous people – from the Theatre Royal. Mike and Bernie Winters used to sell stockings here before they started in pantomime. In the fifties the Market was open on Saturday until nine or ten to catch the people going to the Theatre Royal or the Hippodrome.

Some of us got rich. It's a starting point for a business. But no one could do it now. It costs far too much to set up. A lot of this is branded stuff.

I'm pleased with what I've done. I was in the right place at the right time.

Richard Anderson, aged 41, looks a lot like his father. He has two children, Robert and Michelle.

I started here when I left school. It's hard work. Long hours. I go to trade shows in Manchester and London. On Saturdays the place would be mobbed, but now there's too much retail – too much development.

## GARETH BUTCHER
## HERBS AND SPICES

With his expressive eyebrows and bristling moustache, there is an air of menace and mischief about Gareth, something of the buccaneer. A Shakespeare, Bible-quoting buccaneer who entertains and disconcerts in equal measure.

**Gareth's is the only place where I'm patient in a queue as the banter is usually worth the wait.** *Diana Heuvel*

He also enjoys Fine Art and plays the guitar in a Blues Band. 'In a Lesbian and Socialist band in Manchester, occasionally.' He has a postcard from one of the band members pinned up and has a sign on his scales. 'Nuclear Power, no thanks. Blues Power, yes please' and Boogie Band. He plays Blues to relax.

Gareth sells a wide range of exotic herbs, spices and whole foods. They are all labelled in his elegant calligraphic handwriting. He knows the use of them all and likes cooking for his family. 'Curry is the most popular food in Britain, but I can do a roast as well.' He also knows his botany. 'Black peppercorns are from the piperium family, which is different from the capsicum family...'

**The stall started in 1973 with three boxes of fruit working two days a week. It wasn't a lock-up then. I'm not bothered by the health food shops. My stuff is fresher, cheaper, more varied. There's no packaging, which makes it a hard working life, but you can get any quantity you want of anything. I've had different suppliers: a warehouse in Southgate, then Euston, now Park Royal.**

**I was brought up in Nottinghamshire. My father was a captain in a Baluchi regiment in India and speaks fluent Urdu ('the esperanto of India'). There were lots of Asians in Nottingham even in the fifties. There'd be a knock on the door. Itinerant salesmen. Gabardine mac and a turban. My dad would invite them in, sit them down in an armchair and have long conversations in Urdu while they smoked Senior Service.**

Customer on Gareth's stall: 'Some herbs Provençal please.'
Gareth: 'How many?'
Customer: 'Ooh. A handful.'
Gareth: 'How big is your hand?'
Customer holds his hand up.
Gareth: 'Mine's this big.' (Gareth's is twice as big.)

**I buy from Gareth. He knows what I want. His hand hovers over the figs and he says 'These, I presume', without looking at me. He tries to get us to order in kilos. 'That's the law,' he says. So I just ask for £3.30 worth of figs please. He has a way of talking to one person while serving another. Some people find that disconcerting.** *Michael Everitt*

**I was waiting on Gareth's stall. All I wanted was parsley and apricots. But the queue was so long and the chatter went on ... and it got dark! This chap asked for black beans. 'You don't want black beans,' said Gareth. 'They'll ferment in your pocket. You want black curd beans.'** *Diana Heuvel*

## TIM FUTTER
## CANDLE STALL

Tim is busy on his mobile phone. He is a new breed of entrepreneurial stall-holder, running several other businesses as well. He sells all kinds of candles and at this time of year has one on display in a pumpkin head.

I do all sorts of things. I've done Bed and Breakfast in Yarmouth and run a restaurant in Thailand; I've got a degree in English Literature and I'm studying for an MBA (a Masters in Business Administration); I've written a couple of books and a few short stories. At the moment I'm writing a dissertation on 'The Valuation of Intangible Assets'.

## LIAM MURPHY
## THIS AND THAT

On the last Saturday before Christmas Liam is serving 'Mulled Wayne'. (Recipe: cranberry juice and water 50/50; cloves; juniper; mace; cinnamon; orange; lemon; grapefruit; and pomegranate.) Very good.

I may be here on New Year's Eve, making money merry-making. I sell Aeolian wind harps; string vests; bluebottles; bee and bird boxes; chinese scooters; and CDs. I'm looking for a new line … And I've just been writing a novel in 24 hours at the Norwich Gallery.

## CHRIS CROWE
## FRESH FISH

There's a smiling photo of Chris above the counter with a grimacing shark. Also pinned up are photographs of his two sons and of George Howard, who started up the stall 27 years ago and whose niece, Brenda, still works there. This kind of personal continuity is part of the charm of some of the market's more established stalls. Chris is shiny, polished, boyishly cheery. He sells a wide variety of fresh fish from cod's cheeks to smoked salmon trimmings.

**I bought this stall ten years ago but I've worked here for eighteen years. We get lots of fish from Lowestoft – plaice, skate, lemon sole, dogfish, herrings – delivered fresh three times a day. But in the winter you can't rely on them so much so we buy from Grimsby, Hull, Scotland – even America. There are deliveries at Heathrow and Gatwick three times a week. The mussels come from Stiffkey, or Mawston, the cockles from Dorset. I've got 47 different varieties on my stall today. Fish is becoming popular again, but the English still think of it as a cheap meal.**

**They're prepared to pay more on the continent. My prices vary of course – supply and demand. A lot depends on the weather.**

**I was the first to have a shark on my stall. Here's a picture of a swordfish I had flown in. It went in two days. Mine isn't much of a passing trade. Most of my customers are regular. People bring their children, who in turn bring their children, and they bring their children.**

We're interrupted by Paul Denny, in a blue overall, with a fresh delivery from Lowestoft. I buy red mullet for supper.

## JOE SILVESTER
## PET ACCESSORIES

Squeaky chops and rubber pigs. Cowhide chewy shoes. Chewy Christmas crackers. These are just some of the things Joe sells on his pet-accessory stall. His two sons, Ben, 28, and Justin, 30, run the stall. Joe gave me such a long and fascinating interview, but little remains of it here. You will find it sprinkled throughout the book.

**I've been on the market for 25 years. In those days we would start at five in the morning and be sold out by two. Now, my boys are here at six o'clock in the morning. They have a cup of tea and a bacon roll. There are lots of blue jokes – all innocent because there's no one around to hear them. I help my boys sometimes. Other times they give me £25 to go away because I drive them crackers.**

**Some people complain. They say they can't get up the alley-way. So why are the chips sold out by two o'clock?**

**It used to be easy to get a stall. All you needed was something to sell. But now you need business plans. Investment. A lot fall by the wayside. It's the survival of the fittest.**

## J. & R. ELLIS
## SECOND-HAND BOOKS

Matthew Ellis spoke to me. His brother Peter also works on the stall. Matthew is brisk and business-like and when not serving is constantly tidying and sorting. The promisingly fat paperback books are ranged in neat rows and piles over four stalls.

**The stall was started by my parents in 1957. They have a second-hand bookshop in St Giles where they sell Art, History things like that. On the stall we have modern paperback fiction. There are six family members involved: my parents, three brothers and a sister. I started at 16, though I was in frozen food for ten years. Yes, I do read the books, so that I know what to recommend to my customers. I get to know what they like and put them by. I read practically anything. The most popular authors here are the most popular anywhere: Catherine Cookson, Stephen King, Romantic. We get them from lots of places – house clearance, auctions, or customers bring them in. Not so many from remainders these days as books are now produced especially for the remainder market and they're not so good. We pay cash or they exchange one lot of books for another, a kind of recycling. We've got a hard core of regular customers. From October to April it's the regular local trade, from May to September the tourists. We generally sell at half the published price. The net book agreement hasn't really affected us. Winter is a struggle.**

I try to talk to Matthew's brother Peter, who is deaf like me. But I rely on lip-reading, whereas Peter, who has been profoundly deaf from babyhood, is a signer, so our conversation was limited. Ironic that the deaf are unable to communicate with each other since they speak different languages!

## MIRIAM BOWGEN
## CARY'S FLOWER STALL

This picturesque corner of the market is one of the first things the visitor sees. It is a family business started by Donald Walter Cary. Margaret Cary works there and his son Stephen. Miriam Bowgen, a sister, also works there. They have run the stall since 1974.

The 'twins' work here, two young men with a great sense of occasion – they are wearing Father Christmas hats and tinsel. They work hard and never look you in the eye. I'm told that they only way to tell them apart is that one is a Norwich and the other an Ipswich supporter.

**The problem with flowers is that you need to sell them quick. More men buy flowers nowadays: they wouldn't do that in the old days. The flowers come from all over the place – Scotland, Lincolnshire, Cornwall, Jersey.**

**The customers are usually honest. I gave someone change for a £10 note instead of £5. They gave it back. It's nice to be honest. I'd like the stall to go on for the next generation. I've got no regrets.**

## NEIL HUME
## CITY SCENTERS

Neil wears a gold earring and lifts his cap a lot to scratch his head. He is from Yarmouth but now lives in Diss and has had the stall for four years. He sells a selection of 'new age' objects, oils and oil-burners, ornaments, paintings on velvet, crystals, dream-catchers – circular arrangements of feathers and beads. He says he believes in 'a bit of everything and nothing', and his stall reflects this. I ask him how the dream-catchers work.

**They catch your bad dreams. Then they evaporate with the sunlight in the morning. They're made in Hong Kong and Mexico. I don't have one myself. But I believe in the power of the mind. I've only got to think about people and they appear. I've only got to think about the sun and it comes out. See that bear there? It's a symbol of togetherness in a family.**

**I used to work for an engineering firm. After twenty years of loyal service they just booted me out of the door. I couldn't work for anyone else now. I've been ill for a while. It's great to be back. I love the atmosphere here. There's not much chance to get bored. If I haven't got any customers I shuffle stuff about or go for a walk. I wish I'd done it years ago.**

## JAMES GOWING
## MIKE'S HABERDASHERY

James is 80 years old. He stands smiling behind the trailing ribbons, tapes, sequins, buttons, trimmings, velcro, elastic, lace, zips, hooks, eyes, curtain rings. Mike, the stall-owner, is from Yarmouth. James works here three days a week.

**My stuff is much cheaper than the shops. It's more of a laugh as well. I was a baker for 35 years. I was in charge of deliveries to fifteen pubs in Norwich, so I don't want to sit at home. I talk a bit fast I do. I've always been fast at everything I do. I don't use the phone. I can't understand why people need phones. Why don't you just go and see the fella? I like to be face to face. Keep things simple.**

**I'm a happy-go-lucky sort of fella. If people get at me I say 'I can't stop now', an' off I go. On the move.**

A customer comes along. 'Curtain time is it?' says James.

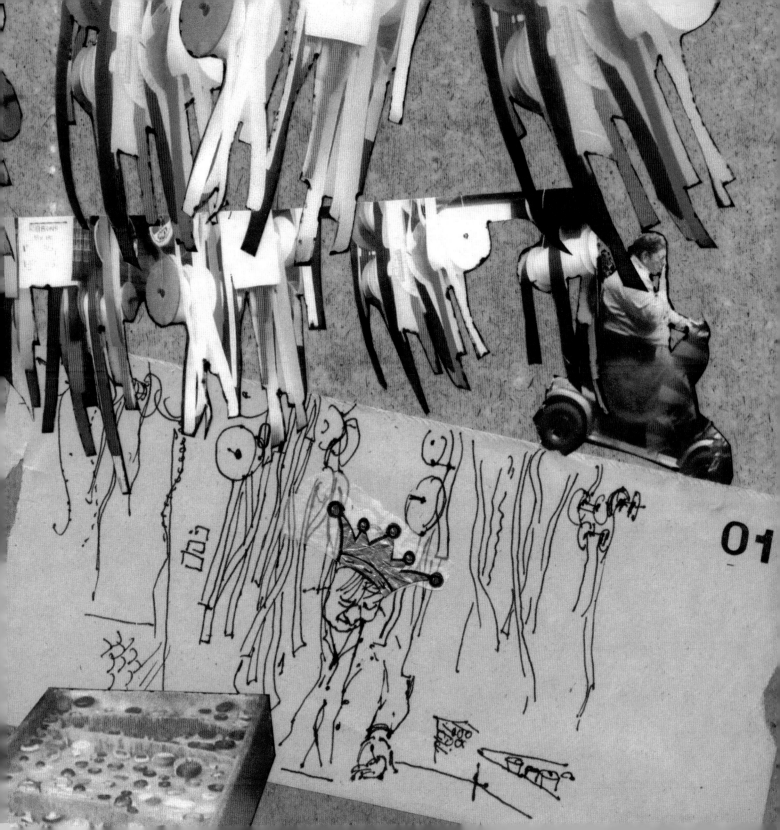

01

## JOHN KETT
## ROOTS AND FRUITS

John is a descendant of the famous rebel Robert Kett. He has an oval face and soft, pleasant Norfolk features. His stall is one of several for fruit and vegetables.

I've run this stall for fourteen years – third generation. My grandmother started in Great Yarmouth selling rabbits. One day someone came along with a box of oranges to sell. It went from there to everything in the orchard. I left school at 17. I worked in the building trade for ten years but used to help my grandma when a lad. I was in the Royal Navy for eighteen years. I've travelled – seen the way other people live, seen wealth, seen poverty. I used to be an admiral's chef. I saw Prince Charles's wedding cake and Prince William's christening cake. I was in the same squadron as Prince Charles when he was on a minesweeper.

I like it on the market. You meet all kinds of people. Time go ever so quick. People bring their children to the stall, and their children bring their children. It's not so good when there's no one around.

People say some strange things. They'll ask you for a kilo of potatoes, 'only make them small so they won't be so heavy to carry home'. Or they pick up a turnip, which are all a bit green, and ask me for a ripe one. Are the grapes sweet? Are the pears soft? If so, they don't want them.

I don't do organic vegetables. They don't present well. They look tired and dirty. Most of my vegetables come from Norfolk. Other things from the wholesalers. I'm up at six every morning and I work till six.

## ARTHUR AND PAUL (JUMMA) HUNT
## CASUAL WEAR

Two brothers, both short, one amiable, inquisitive, the other with fiercely bristling white hair and a slight air of outrage, but equally amiable. They put me in mind of two small furry animals.

I started here when I was 10 years old. Our father was a fish merchant. We used to help our mother with the cockles and mussels. We've had the current stall for 40 years. I've known my dad start the week with half a crown in his pocket and end up with a £1. I once didn't take a penny in eight days. And you've still got your expenses to pay. I've lost a lot of money. Big money. But you have to take the good with the bad. Not easy.

Even after all this time, it's difficult to know what the customers want. If you try to be helpful, some people feel harassed. If you leave them alone, they feel ignored. You can't tell which is which. Sometimes people ask you for something – combat trousers say, and walk off while you're looking for it. But I like the environment on the market. There's lots of laughs. The things people say. *Paul (Jumma) Hunt*

I used to be a milkman. After that a lorry driver. I'm retired now. My lad, Adrian – he's 35 – he runs the stall now.

The public can be difficult. They change their minds. One fella brought back a sea-fishing suit. He said one of the buttons had gone rusty. I said to him, 'The bloody sea rots battleships, never mind buttons!' He went to the small claims court. When the magistrate heard that our suit cost £10, instead of the usual £50, he found in our favour. The public know their own rights, but they don't think we've got any. Ninety per cent of people are lovely, but 10 per cent are rude. Marks and Spencer's set a bad precedent by allowing people to take things back. We get people who buy things, wear them for a weekend, then bring them back and want a refund. *Arthur Hunt*

Arthur and Paul gave me list of excuses customers offer for not making a purchase:

'I'll be back. '        'It aint for me.'        'I'm just going to the bank to get some money.'

''S for my neighbour.'        'Are you here every day?'        'See you on Saturday.'

'Well, we know you're here.'        'Will you keep that one for me?'

'It's not for me. But I'll tell 'im.'        [Big people] 'You can't fit me!'

## CHRIS LANCASTER
## NEWSAGENT

Chris's stall is on the Guildhall side of the market. There are four stalls in all, also selling giftware and souvenirs – at this time of year it's Merry Christmas tea towels. Eight members of the family are involved in the work. In the early mornings the old boys gather round and discuss world affairs over their newspapers.

**It's lovely here. Relaxed and friendly with lots of banter. It's hard work. I get up at 5.30 every day and I'm not back until 6.30.**

Dawn Lancaster is pleasant, round-faced, fair hair, peaches-and-cream complexion, big smile, white teeth. A very kindly manner. As wholesome as apple pie.

**My mum used to work here when she was little. The stall used to be open when the pubs shut. They'd shove her on a box and she had to shout. I wanted to do something different. I went to work in a solicitor's at first but I wasn't earning enough. I left without telling my Mum and went to the shoe factory. I met Chris in 1988. His aunt and my mother used to go dancing together. We lived in Dartmoor for a while. But now I couldn't live anywhere else but Norwich.**

**It's hard work but people get discouraged too easily. They need to change their views. We've gone into touristy things to survive.**

Kristy – daughter of Chris and Dawn – is a student at Norwich City College. She has been working on a project on the Market. From this I learnt the following:

There are between 800 to 1000 people employed to help run the market. The number of fruit and vegetable stalls has been significantly reduced because of the supermarkets. New commodities such as pet food, cosmetic, toe and heel bar, hair-dressing, and watch repair have taken their place, to name but a few.

There are 205 fixed, locked stalls. All the market-traders pay rent, varying from £180 to £500 a month. The market is open six days a week but most of the stalls open on Sunday in the run up to Christmas.

## JERRY BOLWES
## (part of MALCOLM'S MEDIA MINE)

Jerry's stall is a treasure trove of cultural bygones – old records, comics, magazines. *Picture Post* with Brigitte Bardot 1955, *Beezer Express Annual*, Dylan Thomas's *Under Milk Wood*, old Elvis records, Tommy Steele, *The Duke Wore Jeans*, Goon Show Classics, *Billy the Kid Western Annual*, Anti Nowhere League, Wombles, Doris Day, Sex Pistols. So many of the cultural icons of the last 50 years.

**I'm Malcolm's son-in-law – or son-outlaw sometimes. We've been here twenty years. People on holiday in Norfolk come here. 'We didn't think we'd get that anywhere and you've got one,' they say. But they sell a lot of these things on the Internet now and at auction.**

## BRIAN PICKERING
## PICKERING'S SAUSAGE STALL

Red and white tiles. Sausages on a string. Sausages by post. Thai sausages, Polish sausages, diet sausages, gluten-free sausages, Northumberland sausages, all made by Brian in Norfolk. There is a sale on: Buy 2lb sausages get 1lb free.

Brian has white teeth and a fresh, rosy complexion. The blue of his eyes reflects the turquoise of his jumper. He looks as spick and span as his stall. He keeps up with the times and has his own website.

The stall has been here for 42 years. We've also got two shops. My wife usually runs the stall. I've only worked here for a short while so I can see it as an outsider. It's brilliant! Incredible! The people that come here! The powers that be don't realise how unique Norwich Market is. I talk on Radio Norfolk sometimes. People pick it up in Huddersfield. I get people from Yorkshire waving at me when they visit.

I make all my own sausages. I make the pork pies and the pickerami, and the pork cheese – that's a kind of brawn. I cure and smoke my own bacon. Yes, I make the cabanas. My love in life is what I can do with meat. No, I don't supply restaurants. I can do in tens, but not in hundreds.

They have fish sausages in Holland. With advice from a German firm I'm producing them here. All the proceeds go to *Children in Need*. The fish burgers I made were very popular.

I've just been shopping on the fish stall. I bought mussels, whelks and Stiffkey blue cockles, which are the best. Where else can you buy such a variety of fresh seafood at three in the afternoon? I'm making seafood tagliatelli this evening, from Jamie Oliver's cookbook. I love cooking.

What the market needs is something to bring it all together. A focal point. There used to be competitions. I won Retail Butcher of the year four times running which paid for my holidays. In 1987 I won a van.

## LINDA JAMES
## SOCKS & KNICKERS

I've been running this stall for seventeen years. I do one day's buying a month in Nottingham or London. I sell old-fashioned knickers which you can't buy in the shops anymore, long-sleeve thermals, right through to crotchless knickers and thongs. I don't get so many youngsters these days. They all want designer labels. But I've got so many regular customers.

There's always something to do – tidying up, and so on. I come and go when I like, nothing too exciting. Have you seen the Rocky Horror Show which they do at the UEA? The blokes all come and kit themselves out, body stockings, glitter, thongs, bras. Good fun.

People pass the time of day with you on the market. In the shops they're just looking for the next customer.

## MRS M. REID
## SLIPPER STALL

With blue eyes and curly hair, Mrs Reid has an old-fashioned formality. She has a wide range of slippers, including lots of novelties – teletubbies, snails, rabbits, tigers, pandas, ducks. They all look affordable – men's slippers at £3.99, for instance.

I've been here twenty years. I'm not so busy since the Mall opened but there isn't a stall like this there. The trouble nowadays is the parking. It costs £10 a day to use the car-park so that's £60 a week before you've even started. Everyday people, normal people, can't afford that. People say they love the market, but it gets more difficult to make a living. But no matter what you've got, no matter what your stall looks like, you've got to accept change.

I notice in the days after Christmas that the slipper stall is closed. 'There will only be lots of people wanting to change their slippers,' Andy explained. 'It can wait until Saturday.'

## LENNY NIXON
## ARMY SURPLUS

Lenny is a big, friendly man. He has an excellent range of ex-German Army boots, each pair shaped and imprinted by their former owners who stand in a line like ghosts. At £15 they are popular with students.

I've been here 27 years. We used to have a laugh but all the characters are gone now aint they? Why have they gone? I dunno. They're the ones who lived through the hard times ain't they? They had larger families. Times change. It's all commercial now. But everything goes round in a circle. It used to be food on the market, then clothing, now it's going back to food again.

## MALCOLM PELL
## MALCOLM'S MEDIA MINE

Malcolm is mild-mannered, fine-featured. He wears a Breton hat and a tweed jacket, and looks like a handsome seafarer with sanguine complexion, and very blue eyes. His stall is packed with cassettes, records, tapes. Overhead is a sign saying MOIND Y HID BOY! (MAWTHER). Keeping him company is Lassie, a three-year-old bearskin Welsh border collie.

I started off in 1977 in bric-à-brac. Now I deal in all forms of entertainment. Reading the market is important – but I know what people want locally. For instance, if a major artist dies, as Russ Conway did recently, I can respond quickly. This stall is the culmination of a lot of experience. I did years in retail distribution for the Co-op. I realised that people were going to have much more leisure time and that's what I cater for: videos, computer games, tapes, records, CDs.

I've got a website, but the mobile phone has made the real difference. Contacting people at a moment's notice. But we've all had a lean time since the library burnt down and the electricity board moved. People would call in on the market when they were changing a book or paying a bill.

My wife's a freelance journalist. She did an English degree at UEA. My degree is in humanity. The market is the hub of the city.

I'm fascinated by these people. They've really got their own dialect. It's a long process to become part of it. You have to make an effort.

He stops to give a tape he has specially made for a customer because his 'wife isn't well'.

## JIMMY COSSEY
## ELECTRICAL

Amongst other things this stall sells catalogue returns and factory reconditioned goods. He hints darkly at a shady past but won't supply details. Jimmy owns the stall but is only here on this occasion to 'keep his hand in'. I feel I've missed my chance here with 'the dark stuff'.

## JANE SPANTON
## BAGS PLUS

Jane is smiling, blonde, pretty. Her pale lilac fleecy jacket looks well with the vase of pink carnations by the till. She sells bags of all kinds and qualities: leather, canvas, tapestry, silver, gold, 'unique, locally made carpet-bags, each one an individual'. Practical, positive and cheerful, she sees her stall as a business challenge. Her friend, Tracy, who used to work on the market has joined her for a cup of tea. A notice on a beam overhead says 'Duck or grouse'.

I've been here for thirteen years. I started with one stall and built up to three. I used to have a shop but now I've got used to being in the open air. In those days the stalls used to fetch a lot of money. Now quite a few of them are empty. You get a good cross-section of people. They come to me because they get the same quality as they do in the big stores but cheaper. You can get those bags in Liberty's, those in Bond's. They come from the same suppliers.
Of course, I enjoy it. I don't see the point of doing something day in, day out, that you don't enjoy. The market is one of the few places where you've still got independent retailers. In the High Street they're all multiples.

## ALEXANDER POND
## POND'S FLOWERS

Alexander is red-haired, eager, boyish, blue-eyed and very willing to talk. His youthful looks belie his years. As well as selling bouquets and plants from the front, the stall caters for weddings and funeral tributes.

Pond's is one of the original stall-holders. We've been here for 200 years. My father. My brother. My father's mother. My father's mother's mother. My father died of a heart attack when he was 49. My brother died of asthma last year. We're related to Pond's shoes. There's still a shop in Castle Meadow.

People don't communicate these days. They walk around as if they've got a weight on their shoulders. They sit on a seat by themselves, apart. It's because they've all got too much. I had to work hard. I had a paper round. My father said, 'Tell the truth and work hard. Then you'll get on in life.'

But children nowadays – playing all these computer games. I take my children tadpoling, conkering, bird-nesting. I still get excited when I see a really big conker.

I liked Margaret Thatcher. She was a proper woman. She did what she said she'd do. Women rule the world. Why? Because they've got bodies. And men want their bodies. So they'll always rule the world.

The 'lovely Pat' walks by and picks up a eucalyptus tree from his display. Holding it all the while, she joins in the conversation. She agrees with his view on modern youth. 'I'd close down half the Universities. All this sociology. All this nonsense.' Alexander gives her the white china pot holder for the tree. 'He's so sweet and kind. We often talk.'

He gets his flowers from the wholesaler at Harford Bridge: R. N. Gidney. 'He send 'em up cos he know how I think,' he says in his 'purr Norfolk' accent.

I was born in Dereham road. Opposite the cemetery. I did all sorts in that cemetery.

I love my flowers. I learn something different ever day. We don't get the seasons anymore but I do with my flowers. I'm 90 per cent happy. Ten per cent stress. I worry cos I'm self-employed. I haven't had a holiday for five years. You know what men are – think the world can't go on without them. But I'm taking the family abroad next year. Southern Spain. Or to Loch Ness.

He doesn't have much waste with the flowers. 'Only in the summer, when it's 80 degrees. Then I have to throw them in the bin.'

There's one woman has been coming here for 38 years – a pensioner. Every week she spends £20 on flowers. Whatever the weather. To put on graves. One day she sat over there and someone took her bag. I want to wrap her up in cotton wool. She does the same thing every week. Buys her flowers. Sits over there, smokes a cigarette, looks up at the sky. Then with a sharp wave over her shoulder she's gone.

Do you know Alex Pond? The Flower-man? I asked him one day if I could leave my shopping with him until I was ready to pick it up. That was years ago. I've been doing it ever since.
*Alfy Williamson*

## DAVID RIDGEWAY
## BAGS AND BELTS

David's Stall is in the Haymarket. He has a friendly, weathered face, piercing blue eyes behind his glasses, devils' whisker eyebrows and a curly fuzz of grey hair.

I've worked here for eighteen years. I hope to retire one day. We're out on a limb here but I don't mind. I'd find it too claustrophobic in the main bit. But I wish my stall was a lockup. I have to set it up and take it down every day. Takes me about 40 minutes. It isn't the same as it was. Trade isn't so good today but we were run off our feet yesterday.

Later, David hands me a long poem about the market written in the same metre as 'Hiawatha'.
'Is it original?' I ask. 'Has it been published before?'
He grins. 'I just wrote it the other evening because you asked. Whatever comes into my head. I like messing about with poems.'
It is a dark piece, about a crow perched on the Mancroft, watching the activities of the people down below and waiting for their souls to float skywards where he snatches them in his beak. It isn't possible to include it all, but here is an extract:

High above the black crow watched
From his lonely vantage on the Mancroft
With hooded eye that blinked and saw
All the dealings down below
Beneath the shelter of the rainbow
Coloured canvas covered grimy rooftops
The traders did their daily dealings
Daybreak saw the gangways throb with life
Left behind the gloomy darkness
And all the creatures of the night
The rats and mice and vampire bats
The roaches, slugs and worms and things
Flew and scurried to the safety
Of their little nooks and crannies
Where they slept the daytime through
Smells of coffee, tea, eggs and bacon
Wafted gently to the nostrils
Of the cannibals a-feasting.

## ANDY WORMAN
## THE LEATHER-MAN

Just follow the smell of leather to find Andy or 'the leather-man' as everyone calls him. Andy's stall is crowded with highly decorated bags, purses, hair ornaments, bracelets, belts, scarf woggles. There is a patterned-bedspread canopy overhead and esoteric objects dotted around. A green man peers from a pile of purses. In a beautiful round leather box that he made himself are some of his tools. He is small, bearded, sweet-faced, and wears a checked cap on his curling grey hair It is hard to spot him at first amongst the jumble of goods. You think there might be elves amongst them. He looks quite like an elf himself. He is sewing a heavy duty metal zip into a well-worn black leather jacket. He does all kinds of repairs. Andy also sells a selection of cards called Norfolk Nuggets, taken from his own photographs.

**I've had my stall for 27 years. I buy the leather in London once a year. I make everything myself in my workshop at home in Lakenham, sometimes in the morning before work, but I've got other things to do in the evening. Before that I was a primary-school teacher in London. I did that for three years which was long enough.**

**I see it as just a job. I've just finished doing a degree in fine art at Norwich Art School. I did sculpture and printmaking. But I don't know how anyone makes a living at it. I kept the stall going while I did the degree which meant a bit of ducking and weaving. Yes, I do like it here. My friends come to see me. I've got no particular ambitions. I didn't think I'd be a leather-man when I grew up. It just happened. I don't earn much. But I don't want anyone coming and telling me how to earn more.**

A young man with biker jacket and badges comes along. He wants the badges stitched on to a leather waistcoat. It is very dark and cold. 'Too late now,' says Andy sweetly. 'But bring it tomorrow and I'll do it for you.' A red-haired girl comes along and sniffs the goods. She holds a slide next to her hair for her boyfriend to admire then follows him as he walks away.

## ARCHIE STAGG
## FOAM RUBBER

Archie wears a tartan cap and a leather jacket. He has a gravelly voice and a glint in his very blue eyes. The stall is piled high with foam rubber in different thicknesses and bean-bag fillings.

**This stall has been around for 40 years – since 1960. People use the foam rubber for all kinds of things – making headboards, cushions, padded coat hangers, and so on. But it has to be all flame-retardant now. I've worked here for eight or nine years. I worked for a firm in Glasgow for 21 years. There aren't as many people as there used to be. It could do with a lick of paint. This stall hasn't been painted for two years.**

# ALAN TROWER
## CHEESEMAN

The cheese stall, in the middle of the market, is one of the best known and most popular. Apart from a wide variety of cheeses, Alan sells wonderful olives and a fine display of decorated cheese dishes from the Jean Knowles pottery. With his red hair, neat beard and muslin complexion, Alan is Portuguese Jewish. He looks a born cheeseman.

How did I start up? In 1957 I did the European trip on my motorbike. On the cobbled streets of Pisa, Italy, I saw a little old man pushing a wheelbarrow piled high with cheeses. He was small, round, with a blue apron and a little moustache. It was a hot day and the smell attracted me. It also attracted others. I was 18 then and a virgin. Out of the houses came all these strapping, voluptuous women, and he was hugging them and pinching their bottoms. That's the way to do it, I thought.

It took me a while to get round to it. I did twenty years in London in photography and for ten years ran a general stores. Then I did the self-sufficiency bit. I had goats and pigs. I read up how to skin pigs, but I couldn't skin them. Pigs are loving and giving. Feed them properly and give them a cuddle and they're anybody's. I was working twelve hours a day being self-sufficient and in two years I went through all my savings. Then my marriage broke up. So I had to think again. So the cheese stall is me rejoining the human race.

Let everybody do their own thing. I never wanted it to be very successful, I just wanted to make a living. I could have had a shop – but people are too much in awe – there's such an expectation of knowledge. It's taken me years to help people understand cheese. It's part of our heritage. And people want to hang on to the traditional way of buying – the social exchange, and so on.

Where do I get my cheeses? I poke around in France and Italy, find a supplier, order direct. I offer a wide variety sold with care and love. Ninety-five per cent of my clientele know what they want but some are prepared to push the boat out and try something new. My stall is in the middle of the market. It used to be a dead area. Not any more.

Paula Taylor helps Alan on the cheese stall:

I know most of the customers and what they want. I've found my vocation in life. Cheese. But I only nibble on the low-fat ones.

I leave with some herbed olives, a piece of wonderful dark mature Gouda and unpasteurised Double Gloucester. I'm a little less afraid, much more understanding, of cheese!

Sadly, Alan died six months after this interview.

## PAUL ZACHARIADES
## KOJAK'S BARBERS

My dad's Greek, but I was born in Norwich. I go to Athens. My Uncle Paddy had three barber's shops. I've been here for three years. I had proper training – André Barnard from Topshop. I love it here – the community spirit. I like hair. I like people. I can do any haircut you like. I get asked for the odd Mohican. People rarely complain if they don't like their haircut. You can just tell by the look on their face. I got a druggie came in here one day. She had a great pile of filthy, matted hair. I told her to go home, and wash and comb it before I could cut it. You sometimes get fights. One guy came in with two black eyes. He was a farmer who'd had a fight with the landlord at the Red Lion. Something about a wallet and a Rolls Royce.

## THERESA WRIGHT
## ICE-CREAM

I like it here. I'm in my own little world, but I see a lot. The rubbish collection. Leaves. Trollies. Smells. Pigeons. Delivery vans. I get up at six in the morning, and I'm up and running by 7.45. Every day.

## COLIN STEPHENSON
## NATURAL MEDICINES, HERBAL REMEDIES

Colin looks like an apothecary, studiously preoccupied on his stall, peering through his glasses. He has a quiet manner and a twinkly, round face.

We've had a shop in Exchange Street for 25 years. The stall's been here for eleven. We sell the same things but slightly cheaper. Natural remedies don't work like drugs. They can't do any harm. We treat all sorts of things. Varicose veins, aches and pains, you name it. Echinacea – that boosts the immune system. And of course we give free consultations. That takes a lot of time.

## IAN WOODS
## JEWELLERY

Ian sells lots of jewellery, watch straps and batteries, and the like. He is brisk and businesslike. He clearly can't see much point in what I'm doing: it all seems obvious to him.

I've been working here for 25 years, since I was twelve. I started off with one stall. I now have seven and I employ six people six days a week. I've had no holiday for ten years. I visit my London suppliers twice a week. I like being my own governor – but at this time of year I'd like a shop.

## 'I especially like a pint of mussels or cockles on Saturday.'

To go from the market to the Castle Mall is to experience something of a culture shock. Instead of the smiles, greetings, banter, gossip, interweaving of the market, people walk along in their own private corridors of space. They look distant, enclosed. They are consuming, but not communicating.

There is now a similar Mall in every major city in England, with the same shops selling the same range of goods, in weather-proofed, sterile surroundings. There is not much to indicate the season and nothing to identify the locality. This is the modern shopping experience, built around customer profiles and commercial forecasts.

It is impossible to construct a profile of the market customer. What they have in common, perhaps, is a willingness to take a chance, enjoy an experience, engage with the unexpected, expose themselves to the possibility of an adventure.

**I just walk around until I get where I want to be. I get a bit lost in-between.** *Beryl Eglington*

**The space is so theatrical. It's like the wings of a theatre or the corridors of a ship. I always get the feeling that something is about to happen.** *Lys Flowerday*

By and large, one can identify an 'upmarket' of fresh fruit and vegetables, cheese, fish, meat, herbs and spices, which is patronised by all classes. There is also a 'downmarket' of cheap clothing, ornaments, tea towels, electrical goods and the like, alongside stalls which sell quality outdoor clothing. The two flower stalls are popular with everyone.

In between there are all sorts of curiosities, an occasional stall selling goods from Vietnam, an Indian stall selling jewellery, bags and decorative wall hangings. There is even an Internet Cafe and a stall that will help you research your family history. There are stalls selling china and ornaments, and others which cater for the tourist trade.

Everyone has 'their market'. For each person it is a different place.

**The cheese stall is very good. The market is good for fresh fruit, fresh flowers, fresh fish. That's what it should be about. The market is also good for key cutting and shoe repairs.** *David Adlard*

Philip Browne runs a designer menswear shop opposite the Guildhall. His parents had a fish and chip shop in Yarmouth. He is charming, roguish, affable, talkative, streetwise, chic and sophisticated. He knows the high life and the low life, and even has a persona for each one. He sees the market and the surrounding businesses as entirely complimentary to each other. He takes me on a walkabout – to show me 'his' market. Lots of people are pleased to see him. There is much teasing and joking about his 'poshness'. 'See yer in a bit,' he calls when he leaves.

I shop on the market. I buy fruit, vegetables, that sort of thing. I get things fixed by Andy, the leather-man, jackets and so on. You should meet Rosie, on fabrics. Absolutely vicious she is. *Philip Browne*

Oh yes, I use the market. It's good for cheese, pasta, vegetables, fish – I especially like a pint of mussels or cockles on Saturday. Gumboots. And once a week I buy flowers for my dear wife. *Alastair Darrock*

I like the watch stall. It's brilliant, really good, really cheap. And if it's something small they wave you away, don't charge you. 'Naa … it doesn't matter. ' But there's always a queue. *Judith Deledicq*

My wife is still working seven years after I retired so I do the cooking from Monday to Friday. I've got my favourite vegetable stall – the one who stays open late. You get a cookery lesson from him. *Michael Everitt*

I buy cheese from The Cheeseman. I'm very partial to his camembert. I buy it three weeks ahead and keep it in the fridge until its sell-by date. Then I take it out and keep it at room temperature for 24 hours. Perfect! *Geoffrey Paterson*

I like the smells on the market, the camaraderie. I buy fish, fruit, vegetables, tea, coffee. *Hugh Ferrier*

I bought my apricot fleecy on the market. I buy bananas here, too. They give them away at four o'clock. The lady on the flower stall. She is so open and kind. She'd do anything for anyone. I'm always buying bits from the plant stall. One year I bought a multi-branched Yucca plant from Broderick Pond. It was ten or twelve feet high. He gave me a lift home with it. I dream about planting. [With Will Giles, she cultivates an exotic mediterranean garden open to the public.] We work in the garden at night, with a spotlight, and owls for company. Will bought me a packet of nasturtium seeds for my twenty-first birthday and I never looked back. *Sandra Pond*

It's just what a market should be. Open every day. You can get Marks and Spencer's duvets there for £5. A French firm made them wrong. *Griff (Kevin Joyce)*

When I need plants for my garden, I rise early and come to the W. I. stall on a Thursday morning. One has to come early as the stall closes by nine o'clock. The only place I can buy that delicious smelly cheese is from the stall here. No shop will stock it as it stinks the place out. *Ros Newman*

I've been coming to the market for twenty years. It was always our 'buy-the-children's-shoes place'. Nowadays, Flo [Rosie's lurcher] always drags me to the doggie bit. They've got things like children's shoes made out of animal hide and all sorts of tasty things.

I like the cheeky flower-boy – the blond one [Alex Pond]. He's got the patter – lots of lip. You can tell it's his life-blood. I also buy my half-rim spectacles from the specs stall. The cheese stall is very good but the poor man there has a permanently bad back from standing on a slope.

And then there's the W.I. stall on a Thursday morning. You've got to be there very early – 8 to 8.30. I always pass off their home-baked as my home-baked. And you can buy cottage-garden plants there which you can't buy anywhere else. *Rosie Inglis*

We like the market. Ain't many markets that are open every day. We wish it was open longer. We buy records, fruit, clothes, sandwiches and stuff. *Kim Dye and Emma Jackson*

My favourite buys:
Chris for the news.
John for the Veg.
Plaice roes from the fish stall.
Pickerings in the middle.
And when I was Lord Mayor, flowers for the parlour.
Long live Norwich market.
*Brenda Ferris, former Lord Mayor*

Go to the card stall for the best foil Christmas wrapping paper! *Sally Kelsey*

Oh yes. I use the market. I used to take my whippet down there. 'That's it. Whip it in, whip it out,' they used to call. *Diana Lamb*

I like the heel bar. They get things done. *Geoffrey Patterson*

Oranges, olives, fluffy slippers, cheese, roses, sparkly tops, sausages, chips, curtains, old people. Walking, passing, looking, chatting, smiling, laughing, vibrant life. The market at Christmas. *Eilean MacGibbon*

I buy my wrapping paper on the market. My son bought me an electric filofax recently. 'All it needs, Mum, is a battery.' I went to every computer shop in Norwich looking for a battery. I went to

Jarrold's. I went to Dixon's. Then somebody said, 'You could do worse than try the market.' So I went to this little watchmaker's stall on the end. He fixed me with a battery, just like that. You can also get the finest cheeses in Norfolk there. *Angela Woodhouse*

I buy flowers, joss-sticks, nuts from the herb and spices man. Not fruit and vegetables. They're too heavy to carry. I sometimes get a reduction on my flowers. *Veronica Clark*

When I was interviewed for the job as secretary organiser of the Norwich Society on May 1st 1991, I was asked: 'If you were stranded on a desert island, what would you think most strongly about in Norwich?'

My answer, naturally, was the Cathedral. But I said I would remember particularly the open market, the flower stalls, Gentleman's Walk, the bustle, the activity, because this is the centre of the city, the hub of its active life. They offered me the job. *Sheila Kefford, Norwich Society*

I get socks, pants, gloves and hats from here. Sometimes records from Jerry. I like the market for its down-to-earthness and easy access. *William Lambert*

Today we bought soap, thermal vests, brussels sprouts, brazil nuts, broccoli and a couple of books. *Susan Curran*

I come for the basics: batteries, tapes, gloves, socks. Loads of my friends come. We go round looking for bargains. Look at these candles I bought. *Francesca Johnson, aged 15*


Roses are red.
Violets are blue.
The market is great.
Especially for stew.
 *John Garret*

Quality tea-leaf tea is available only on the market and in the Assembly Rooms if requested. *Nigel Pointer*

I used to like to have cockles and mussels and a bit of bread for my lunch. Sometimes oysters. But then I got a duodenal ulcer and couldn't have oysters any more. *Colin Self*

Oh yes I use the market. I buy cheese – excellent cheese – and anoraks. I did once buy a toolbox. As I was going to buy cheese afterwards I was thinking out loud to myself that I could carry the cheese home in the toolbox. The stall-holder wagged his finger at me. 'No, It's not a cheese box. It's a tool box. You know. Tools!' *Alan Fry*

For many visitors to the market, the point is not shopping at all:

We don't come here to buy anything. Oh no. We come to hear the Norfolk accent! *Margaret and Cyril Fielder (from Portsmouth)*

I like watching the faces. It's a treat to come into town. *John Childs*

Rapport. That's what the market's all about. Rapport. *Diana Heuvel*

I like listening to the things people say. It makes me smile inside myself. *Joy Alcock*

I love the market because everyone is so cheerful and I always come back. *D. Lambden, aged 13*

We are coming from Israel. Two brothers and two sisters. We have good time here and meet nice people. *Yonat Freudenthal*

I like the market because it's full of lovely people and food and life, and long may it thrive. *Tony George*

We like Norwich market because its aisles are miles of smiles! *Jack and Sylvia Gordon*

**'I could love you in another life.'**

Apart from the customers, there is a whole tribe of people who come to the market just to 'hang out'. The traders call them 'Faces'.

Some make themselves useful, helping out on the stalls, minding them while the stall-holders go on an errand. Others start up their own small enterprise on the side. Others just wander around, striking up a conversation on one of the tea stalls or with whoever they know. Whatever, they can go there for company, connect with other human beings. They are part of the market's colour and character. They don't spend much money, as far as I can see, but are a kind of currency in themselves.

'Ask Tingy about the market,' the traders say to me. 'He knows all there is to know.'

Eventually I find him, otherwise known as Reg. He has white hair brushed back, a coat tied with string, enormous boots.

But Tingy is elusive. He is always striding away – intent and purposeful, disappearing down aisles, rushing round corners. He is like the white rabbit in Alice in Wonderland. 'Find Cutty? Tuccy? Tingy?' I keep scribbling in my notebook.

I catch him one day. 'Are you in a hurry?' I ask tentatively.

'Yes,' he snaps back, and goes on his way.

Then Rosamund, a florist who used to have a stall on the market, tells me about him:

**When the stall-holders arrive with their produce, they used to throw all the boxes aside. Tingy used to collect them all up and store them in a lock-up he had at the back of the market. Then, when the traders needed boxes, he'd sell them back to them. You used to see him sitting on an old bentwood rocker at the front of the market.**

Eventually, after a gap of three years, I spy Tingy leaning near one of the tea stalls. He seems to have slowed down.

'Why do you come here?' I ask him.

He shrugs. 'It passes the time. It's better than staying indoors all day.'

Ah! So that's one mystery solved.

In the summer of 2004 Tingy is often seen on the market, smartly dressed and no longer rushing around, but sitting, watching, whiling away his days as this era of the market draws to a close. What a store of memories he must have! How I wish I could have tapped into them! It is quite a triumph, in his declining years, to be still part of this teeming life around him.

Then there is Harold, who looks like a 1930s Hollywood gangster. He has sleeked back, steely hair and a black overcoat. He wears a hand-knitted fair-isle waistcoat. His hands are conspicuously bejewelled with heavy, ornate gold rings.

**My wife bought them for me. Ruby, sapphire, garnet, onyx, malachite blue. She bought one every Christmas and every birthday. I've got more at home so I can change them round. I take 'em off when I do me 'ousework. I'd spoil them otherwise. She had some rings, too. But she died in 1992. It was Christmas. A Saturday night. I was with her for 36 years. I come into the market every day. I look after Barrie's stall for him if he goes to fix a washing machine or something. Barrie's going to look after my rings one day. 'E says 'e'll keep 'em polished.**

**I used to work on the second-hand clothes stall, 7.30 to 4.00. In between I did my catering. What do I do on Sundays when the market's closed? I cook my dinner and go to bed with my electric blanket.**

The most bizarre looking character is 'Bungay Roger' Harris. He is thin, gnome-like, whiskery. With his rastafarian dreadlocks, hand-stitched leather hat, his denim jacket festooned with badges, he looks a pretty wicked fellow until he puts on a pair of very respectable-looking spectacles. He carries a much-thumbed white Bible in his pocket. 'Read Matthew chapter 21, verse 42,' he tells me: 'The cornerstone of the earth shall be the one that the architect rejected.' He leans forward. 'The cornerstone of the earth is in Norwich.' He seems to have an extended family of children and grandchildren who weave in and out of the market. Abigail, his three-year-old daughter, recites her ABC for me.

**All I've got on me is a pocket full of 'thank you very muchs', another full of 'sorrys'. I've got no money. I'll tell you a story for money.**

**When I was at school we were asked to write down 'things to do in the park'. I wrote, 'Carve on the benches and write on the pavilion'. I was dragged out of the classroom by my hair and given six strokes of the birch. But I was only describing what I saw. I never respected teachers after that. I've always been a bit of an outlaw.**

**I've been convicted for 'riding a pedal cycle furiously' and 'being drunk in charge of a goat'. But a vicar explained to me about people who live conventionally. When the travellers moved into the area, this vicar let them all have a bath in his house. Everybody came. And do you know what. Everybody's car radio disappeared but his.**

**Norwich is being bled to death by carpet-baggers. The community centres have disappeared. The Duke Street centre. The swimming pool. Something's behind it all.**

Jerry greets me one day. "Bungay Roger' came by with part two of his life story. I told him you'd had to go and lie down on account of part one taking so long.'

Some of the 'faces', I suppose, are what is now called 'vulnerable people'. Their talk is not always coherent. Nonetheless, they offer a glimpse into their private worlds and preoccupations.

Rodney was born in 1969. In 1986, when he was 17, he was the victim of a hit-and-run driver and spent six months unconscious in hospital. His spine and legs were injured, and he was brain damaged. His warm brown eyes are intelligent but unfocused. He talks and moves with difficulty. He painstakingly writes down his name as YENDOR, which is Rodney spelt backwards. He has wavy, chestnut-brown hair, curved teeth. He looks very lost, but you can see that this wasn't always so. There is a pocket of lucidity and wisdom in his damaged brain, innocence and sweetness in his face. He survives through begging.

**I've just been an' had one of Sue's bellybusters for breakfast. I hate my job. Do you know what I mean by work? BEGGING! I hate Christmas. It's a waste of money. We're all God. I know so. God smokes a lot. Him Upstairs. What's really killing me – why is God still illegal? I got deported from Amsterdam. How could they deport the disabled King of Europe's Head Beggar?**

He pulls a piece of crumpled paper out of his pocket. 'YOU CAN CLAIM A MILLION POUNDS, HAVE YOU WON TOP PRIZE?' he says. 'Look. I've got a winning ticket. Good, because I've got to give a £100 to a friend to buy a guitar. He'll be able to busk with it. He sells the *Big Issue* at the moment. I call it the Red Issue. You know why? Everyone's read it!'

Rodney kisses my hand. 'I could love you in another life.'

Will Rodney get another life? This one has been sadly marred.

Margaret comes by in a motorised wheelchair. Despite the narrow aisles and the slope, lots of people in wheelchairs use the market. She knows Rodney and is obviously fond of him. She invites him to come and see her in her flat.

'Norwich would be nothing without the market,' she says. 'You get the best cup of tea in the world. And a nice egg and cress roll. You can be matey here, friendly.'

Veronica takes pity on me, shivering in my story-stall. 'Shall I get you a cup of tea and a mince pie?' she offers nervously. She is fragile, elderly, thin. She wears a pair of trousers that are covered in patches made from her deceased father's clothes. She lifts her coat and shows me shyly, like a child with a new dress.

**I come from Sprowston on my moped. The market is my social life. Sometimes I have chips. I like to listen to the gossip.**

Norman approaches one day and with great decorum introduces himself before taking a seat on my stall. He is 70, a retired bus conductor. He wears a trucker cap. He's a born-again Christian and carries his Bible study notes around with him in a black executive briefcase.

**This market's seen a helluva lot. I come every day for a cup of tea and a walk round, apart from Sunday when I go to the King Street chapel.**

**I do Bible studies. People know me here. John [from Roots and Fruits] sent a wreath when my wife died. How would I feel if I couldn't come on the market? Bloody miserable. I'd have nowhere to go. You meet people here. I know him [pointing] and him, and him, and him. But you've got to make yourself known. You can't leave it to other people. I talk to anyone. I make friends easily on the market.**

There is a paradox about the market. It is hard work. It is often hard weather. The men and women who work there are tough on the whole. But, working together as they do, this toughness is transformed into a kind of gentleness, a collective kindness that is totally unpatronising. I can think of no other place where lonely people can drift in and out and yet be so naturally absorbed and accepted.

**'The market's changed. It's spoilt. They've tidied it up too much. They want to tidy it up some more.'**

Supporting the main business of the market is a whole army of delivery men, handymen, carpenters, cleaners. These are the people who work unseen in the twilight hours. Men in red with green machines sweeping up at the end of the day. The bewhiskered, bobble-hatted lavatory attendant with rosy cheeks and no teeth singing into his cleaning cupboard, with only his brushes to hear. These, and many more.

## Neville James (Sadie) – Deliveries

I ask after Sadie. It's 7 a.m. and he's asleep in the lorry. After a while he emerges, tousled, rubbing his bleary eyes. It's too early in the morning to ask many questions.

> I started work on the market in 1952. Fruit and Veg. Now I do deliveries. I left at nine last night and arrived at Spittalfields market at 12.30. I have a cup of tea then buy the fruit and veg. I've just got back from London. So, yes, I work all night. I get some sleep at one o'clock in the afternoon, but only for three or four hours. I'm too tired to sleep longer. I take it easy now. I only do the trip once a week. It used to be three or four times. The market's changed. It's spoilt. They've tidied it up too much. They want to tidy it up some more.

## Harry Southgate and Paul Cromer – Fruit and Veg Deliveries

First thing in the morning. Paul and Harry have been travelling all night but they emerge from their van looking like two fresh-baked buns. They wear immaculate cream jackets with navy trim and look groomed enough for the stage.

> Paul: I've been working here for 50 years – since I was twelve. It's changed. There used to be auctioneers at the back doing their pitch. And the fish market was a lot bigger. I remember the chalk figurines when they first came on the market. Alsatian dogs, and the like. The hygiene's better now but the quality is just the same.

Harry: I was the first to have seamed nylons with a six-inch stiletto heel. I used to look after my girlfriend with nylons. They were hard to get in those days – black market. Coupons. My girlfriend still has a pair in their original packet.

'Do greengrocers go to classes to learn calligraphy?'

**'I wouldn't buy a G-string if it had been hanging out in the rain. It's personal.'**

One day I was in Gentleman's Walk and I stopped to listen to the noise. At first I couldn't work out what it was and then I realised. It was all this – chatter! You couldn't hear the traffic. It was just a cacophony of voices. It was the voices of the traders and the people sitting round on the benches. It was Babel. I like this idea. The exchange of goods, but also this exchange of words – through 200, 300, how many years? Think of the things that have happened there. Didn't the King come to unveil a plaque? It's a place of enormous emotions. *Pat Moon, Writer*

The market is intimate, intricate, crowded. It is a place of human voices. It is possible to wander in there any time and hear snippets of conversation, fascinating fragments. Sometimes one can only guess at the context, others are complete in themselves. If only one could dip into those that have taken place over the centuries.

Here are a few from our times.

Woman to two woman-friends:
'Look at them cards – ten for 50p! Envelopes cost more than that. So if you don't like the cards you could   just chuck 'em away an' keep the envelopes. An' look, they 'aven't just got flowers on them – they've got animals – those'll do for the men.' [Guffaws of laughter from women.]

At the torch and electrics stall:
Young bloke: 'You got a lantern?'
Stall-holder: 'Ain't got a lantern, mate.'
Young bloke: 'Got a flasher?'
Stall-holder: 'See Dave next door. 'E's been done for flashing.'

Woman:
'Huh. That man on the fruit stall. He's so grumpy. He grouses about his bungalow, his wife, the weather. You daren't touch an orange.'
Friend:
'With some of them you can touch whatever you like.'

'What do you fancy for dinner tonight? Shall I get a cauliflower?'
'No, I'm not in a cauliflower mood.'

At handbag stall. Old woman to old couple:
    'I need a new 'andbag. I threw mine in the bin in Elsie's.'

At the flower stall regarding a pot figure:
    'My friend came in an' 'e bought a witch. Have you got any more?'

Passing teenager:
    ''E's 'orrible to me sometimes, my dad is.'

Stall-holder:
    'I said to 'er, "so what d'you want me to call you? Wife? Wife? Wife?"'

A conversation between two men:
    Man 1: 'Anythin' in there any good?'
    Man 2: 'No.'
    Man 1: 'Anythin' at all?'
    Man 2: 'No.'
    Man 1: 'Shall we go 'ome then?'
    Man 2: 'Yeah.'

Woman at the Natural Medicines stall:
    'Have you got a cure for heartbreak?'
    Stall-holder: 'Time.'
    Woman: 'Time? Time? Time kills.'

Man stuffing a bellybuster smacked on back by passing friend.
    'Enjoyin' your breakfast there?'
    'Yeah.'
    'Good boy!'

Fraught-looking woman:
'Where's the sock stall? I keep missing the sock stall. Socks! Socks! Where are you?'

'What can I get yer? 'Ow about some bread and dripping?'
'Naah. My grannie had a heart attack on that palaver. I'll 'ave some of those windy peas. They make yer fuckin' fart like three pounds of carrots!'

'Mmmm. These mushy peas are better than bleedin' Yarmouth's.'

Boy walking away from market:
'They hint got nun.'
Friend: 'They hint got nun wot?'

Artist who was drawing the Guildhall: Stall-holder comes and looks over her shoulder:
Stall-holder: 'Yer want ter come and draw my missus in the altergerther – cor, that 'ud be wuth thousands of pounds, that ud!'
Artist: 'What does she charge for modelling?'
Stall-holder: 'I dunno, but she charge about the 'ouse in the mornin', I can tell yer.'
Artist: 'Is she plump?'
Stall-holder: 'Wo-ho, she got a luverly pair o' Norfolk dumplins on 'er.'

A customer picks up a primitive-looking green vegetable with conical florets.
'What's this?'
'Romanesque.'
'How do you cook it?'
'Steam it, like cauliflower.'
'What's it like?'
'A cross between broccoli and cauliflower.'
'Is it a new invention?'
'No. It's a Victorian, Norfolk grown, back in fashion.'
'Weird.'
'Are you going to try it?'
'I'll think about it.'

The conversion to metric has caused quite a bit of confusion. A customer points to the sprouts.
'Half of those please.'
'Half a pound or half a kilo?'
The customer looks puzzled.
'Half … whatever.'

Woman pushes pram into man's legs.
  Man: 'Could you please be more careful?'
  Woman: 'Go put yer feet in yer pocket!'

He: 'Are you still married to that poor husband of yours?'

Reggie:
  'Hello Margaret. I've just bought a new answerphone and I want to sell my old one. You 'ent got one 'ev you? You can 'ave it cheap.'
Margaret:
  'We've got no need for one, Reggie, cos no one who's ringed leave a message.'

Woman to friend:
  'Look at those singing fish. What a pity our 'Arold's dead. 'E would have loved one of those.'

Elderly gent at fruit-and-veg stall:
  'Got 'ny raspberries?'
  Stall-holder: 'No, mate. Sorry, mate – all gone.'
  Elderly gent pointing at punnets: 'What's those then?'
  Stall-holder: 'Oh, them's tayberries.'
  Elderly gent: 'What's those then?'
  Stall-holder: 'They're from the same farm. Cross between a blackberry 'n' a raspberry. All the flavour of a raspberry 'n' the size of a blackberry.'
  Elderly gent gazes at tayberries: 'Yeh, you're right there. If those were black they'd be the perfect blackberries. Well, I've lived all my life 'n' never heard of tayberries. You learn somethin' every day don't you?'

Man pointing at flowers:
  ''Ow much are they, then?'
Stall-holder:
  '£4.95 for ten.'
Man with shock-horror expression:
  'Stroll on!'

Two girls examining underwear:
  'I wouldn't buy a G-string if it had been hanging out in the rain. It's personal.'

'Do the fruit-and-vegetable sellers mix with the butchers? Do they meet for tea and mushy peas? I expect they smell very different.'

## 'There were so many people that they must have thought it was the King of Norwich who'd died.'

The market is full of ghosts: a whole host of the dead imprinted on the memory of the living. In turn, these ghosts would have remembered others, as far back as can be imagined. The continuity of the place and the fundamental nature of the activities that take place there mean that these ghosts also have a special, communal, presence. They are known as 'characters'. Mention of them is almost always tinged with fondness and regret.

One death in particular is still fresh in many minds.

**Broderick Pond was a character. He was my best friend and I saw him every day for fifteen years. He died on August 17th five years ago. I remember his funeral well. I was supposed to speak for him in the Peter Mancroft. There was a coach load of Japanese tourists there taking pictures. There were so many people that they must have thought it was the King of Norwich who'd died. It's a tradition that we turn all the lights out when the hearse goes by.** *Chris Crowe, Fish Stall*

**In the old days, when a market-trader died they would have a funeral at Peter Mancroft. The hearse would go by and we'd all switch off our lights to show respect. The last person who had a funeral like that was Broderick Pond from the flower stall. He was only 40. I remember when he was born. His father put a big sign up: 'IT'S A BOY!'** *Joe Silvester*

Photographs are a positive reminder for some. Lenny Nixon, of Army Surplus, has a photograph of Mike Winters, the comedian, selling clothing in the fifties. Also of Fred Stone, a 'character' who lived from 1943 to 1988.

**There was Alec Power and dear old Sydney Smith. I used to be Doctor Junk. Why have the characters gone? People become characters to sell things. They haven't the time now. Life's too regulated for them to survive like that.** *Customer on Lenny's Stall*

**I remember Black Frank – an Indian. He used to dress up in feathers and everything.** *David Ridgeway, Bags and Belts*

There were some real characters around. One old lady that used to go to the lavatory and come out with her clothes all tucked into her knickers. *Joe Silvester*

Billy Seaman was a rum un. He used to catch rabbits on the marshes and sell them on the market. *Neil*

There was this old lady who used to go marlin fishing and sell her catch on the market. *Alfie*

Did you get to hear about Billy Bluelight? He used to sell violets from a basket in the walk. He would run a race against the passenger boat to Yarmouth. *Pat Moon*

There were fortune tellers and quack doctors. One guy used to buy boiled beans and dip them in yellow sugar and sell them as a cure for lumbago and rheumatism. People used to swear by them. *Paul Cromer, Delivery Man*

The characters have all gone now. It's not the same. I remember the Mad Bag Man. He used to sell these bags stuffed with newspapers. He'd throw 'em to the ground to show how cheap he was selling them. He became the Mad Swag Man. I don't know what he sold then. *Harry Southgate, Delivery Man*

We lived in North Walsham so travelled to Norwich by train. I remember speaking to Mike and Bernie Winters on the market. It hasn't changed very much really – and I am 63. We always dressed in a suit or coat and wore a hat. Everyone did in those days. I went with my girl friends or sister. Mike and Bernie used to chat us up. Perhaps they thought if they were nice to us we would buy a handbag. Then there was Alf, 'the purse king', who had a son called Lolly. Alf used to call out, 'real continental calf'.
   Perhaps he thought we were green as we were cabbage looking. *Isabel Kingsnorth*

The Purse King was a gifted salesman. He always made a point of persuading potential customers that he was embarrassing himself considerably in offering his goods at such give-away prices. *John Gay*

I remember Alf, 'The Purse King', who always had dozens of lookers round his stall and sold things at a great pace. His accent was cockney which made him a cut above. *Richard Riseborough*

I remember the stall-holder who sold horse meat. The meat was sprayed blue to show that it was unfit for human consumption. One day a lady walked past. 'Watcha Blue Willy,' she shouted. 'Watcha Red Mary,' Blue Willy shouted back. *Barry Guymer*

I can remember at the end of the war, 1944 and onwards, going to the market on Saturday to listen to Alf, the 'Purse King', selling bags, purses, etc. I did once buy a handbag from him. Mike and Bernie Winters were there selling nylon stockings – a new venture! Only available otherwise if you knew an American serviceman! There was also a chap who sold crockery. He used to put a whole tea-set on a large plate and somehow throw it in the air. Down it came. Never did see any of it broken! In 1950 when we were married we bought a china tea-set – six cups and saucers and plates for £1. It was white china with a gold pattern round the top. *Molly Goodyear*

Then there was the bowler hatted man who sold papers. 'Ally Ucker New', he would call out, which meant 'all the local news'. *Richard Riseborough*

My grandfather, Alfred Howes, used to supply the stall-holders with home-grown produce. He was the first person to supply cooked beetroot to the Market, becoming known as 'The Red Beet King'. He was a small, quiet man with a flat cap and pipe. The stall-holders affectionately nicknamed him 'Mouse' and when he died in 1958 there were tributes to him in the Press. *Janet Howard*

I remember the street entertainers when I was a boy. Handcuffs. Chains. Strong men. It's all changed now. *James Gowing, Mike's Haberdashery*

Sometimes, we can hear the living voices of the ghosts:

One day a stall-holder came into James Warner and asked Walter, the manager, how much his tomatoes were.
'One shilling and nine pence.'
'They're only one and six at Macarthy's.'
'Bloody well go to Macarthy's then [knowing they hadn't got any]. These are one and nine.'
'One and six!'
'One and nine!'
'One and six!'
'All right. One and six. Now bugger off.'
When the stall-holder had gone off very happily with his one and six worth of tomatoes, I said to Walter, 'So you gave in then?'
'No I didn't. They're really only one and three pence.'
He'd been in the business for a long while. *Barry Guymer*

Here's a voice from 1946, recorded in *A Norfolk Notebook* by Rider Haggard:

Woman to friend, tucking a Christmas tree under her arm, 'there's only one child this Christmas, and the Lord knows when I'll get the others back again, but I sez to the old man, "We'll have the tree and all, and if there's not much to hang on it, we'll have to do with hope for a trimmin'."'

And another, in 1992:

Get on with each other? Of course we don't get on. I've never heard of a bunch of market-traders who did. But I wouldn't swap this life for a cosy shop. Even when the water freezes in the flower buckets I wouldn't want to be anywhere else. Give me fresh air and a laugh any day. *Broderick Pond*

Glimpses, fragments, images, voices that linger in the mind, a population in themselves. But it's time that transmutes people into characters. The people there now are the characters of tomorrow.

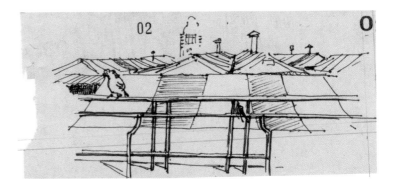

## 'I met my husband on the market. We got married on Valentine's Day.'

The twists and turns of the market, the narrow aisles and unexpected corners, the stalls with their hanging ranks of clothes, make it the ideal place for a flirtatious game of hide-and-seek. Saturday is the day. Groups of teenage girls parade around, chasing, loitering, hanging out, walkie-talking on their mobiles. The market is a maze of flirtation. A boy walks by with half a dead pig on his shoulder. He grins and flirts with three girls and a baby. The baby has a bag of chips and a ketchup face. 'Twas ever thus. A few people have found true love.

I met my partner on the market. She walked by with her long braids and her big fur coat. 'Hello,' I said. 'Hello,' she said. We had coffee together from one of the stalls. We've been together six months now. *Paul Zachariades, Kojak's*

I lived in London for twenty years but Norwich is a much better place for getting to know people. I met my husband on the market. We got married on Valentine's Day. *Beryl Warner*

And for one person at least, the infamous slope had a happy consequence.

My friend Anick was walking through the market one day. It wasn't very busy. She started to sneeze and was tearing a piece off a toilet roll she had bought when she dropped it. Away it rolled, down the slope. A man picked it up. And you know what? She married him. *Eve Stebbing*

January and February are bleak months on the market. It might cheer everyone up to institute this as a Valentine's Day blind date. One sex at one end of the market with their toilet rolls. The other sex at the other end. Your date is at the other end of the roll!

To market, to market, to buy a prime stud,
Home again, love again, this one's a dud.
To market, to market, to buy a young man
Home again, love again, quick as I can.

*Jenny Morris*

**'Other cities would give the earth, sell their souls for a market like this.'**

The market is a magnet. On its fringes, all sorts of people run their own operations: there are 'unofficial' stalls selling organic soaps, organic vegetables, jewellery. There's a motley range of musicians – Peruvian bands, Chinese fiddlers, penny-whistle players, bagpipers – throughout the year. As far back as 1533 records show that an order was given to the City Waits that '... every Sondaye at nyte and other hollydays at nyte uppon the nether leades of the gyildhall and betwixt the howrres of vii and viii of the clock blowe and play uppon their intrements the space of half an howrre to the rejoicing and comforte of the herers therof'. This continued except in times of plague until 1629, and a spate of sabbatarian laws. Another man was given leave to perform 'greate feates with his mouth'. We can only conjecture what they were.

We no longer call them 'strolling players', the market is no longer the setting for the mystery plays, but there are performers and artists of all kinds, in an ever unfolding pageant.

Saturday especially sees balloon-sellers, kite-sellers, soapbox preachers, petition gatherers, market researchers, recruiters for motoring organisations, scavengers. At four o'clock, when the carnival is over and the vegetable stalls are closing, one old lady comes by, hunched over the pram she uses to gather up the left-over produce.

### Paddy

Paddy is not part of the main market but sells flowers outside Habitat. He has a round, rosy face and a gold tooth:

Most of the flowers come from Holland. I get up at three in the morning to be at Halford Bridge livestock market at four o'clock to buy them. On Mother's Day I get up at two. When I sold fruit I used to go off to London at eleven at night to buy and I wouldn't be home until 6.30 the following evening. People don't know that. They think we just stand here. There's these young girls coming into work at nine o'clock and think that's early. We've done four hours work by then.

I used to be a bookmaker. Now I trade in anything. You've got to sell yourself. You've got to be cheerful and chat even if people don't buy the flowers.

A woman comes along and makes a selection for a bouquet. Paddy makes a big bow out of white florist's ribbon – snipping and tying and teasing into shape. The blue and white bouquet of daisies, lilies and chrysanthemums costs £10. It is an armful.

## John (aka Pablo Picasso – World Famous Pavement Artist)

John sits in the middle of one of his large paintings. It is a copy of John Atkinson Grimshaw's *Angel*. He works methodically on the flesh tones of the angel's thighs. Her wings are there in outline. John is a small, thin man, dressed in black, with a dark beard and pony tail. He looks fragile. He smiles a lot when he talks. He has intense blue eyes. There are two hats by his side, both containing a few coins. Passers-by stop frequently. They stare, scowl, study the paintings. Above Richard Dadd's *The Fairy Fella's Masterstroke* there is a sign saying 'Not for Sale'. It is a vivid piece of work, very skilful, and he gets lots of enquiries. Other painting are by the Pre-Raphaelites. *The Blind Girl* by John Everett Millais, *The Last of England* by Ford Madox Ford, *Scapegoat* by William Holman Hunt.

I don't like working in the studio. I feel safer with people. I like the background noise. The music. The talk. The positive energy. Alone in a studio there's no inspiration. Nothing. I paint in acrylic. No, the rain doesn't affect it too badly. There are a few marks here, look' [he points to the angel's thigh]. I don't worry about people walking over them. They don't. Once, I was in Newcastle working outside the football ground. United lost. They were relegated. The crowd came swarming out of the football ground – really angry. But they walked round the paintings, not over them. Lots of them made nice remarks. I lost all fear after that.

I've got cerebral palsy – down my left side. I've got no family – just me – and a computer. I lived on a boat for four years, but now I've got a flat. I went to Art School at Stoke-on-Trent. I've been all over the place, but then I came to Norwich and I liked it. Do I feel like a beggar or a painter? It's a balance. I tell people about Art. I've done different jobs. Social work. Care Assistant. Youth Worker. That sort of thing. I wish I had more to give but I've got this. Sometimes, I wish I could watch the people watching me.

I don't mind if people don't give me money. I'm happy for them to do what they do. I'm happy in my square, in my painting. That's where I've lived for the past ten years. In a painting.

## John Patchett

He is an artist, working in pastels.

I've been painting the market for years. What do I like about it? The trees, the mood, the bustle, the spirit. The striped canvas awnings, the feel and the sound of the place. It's where people meet. So many cities have stripped out the character and traditions. Norwich is one of the few places that has some left. But we don't learn from our mistakes. Look at the Forum. There's no view of the

Assembly Rooms, and from the Assembly Rooms there's only a brick wall. I've heard about the market plans and they are so bland. They're talking about units, buildings, pretend metal awnings. It will be like a coloured car-park. They've got to find a balance between keeping it clean and keeping it alive. Other cities would give the earth, sell their souls for a market like this. But the trees – the lovely plane trees – are dying.

**'And we've got to make sure we end up with a real market – not a civic award-winner!'**

It is inevitable that something so quirky, so wayward and so instinctively anarchic as the market should have to be contained by the authorities. Supported by a team of planners, regulators, inspectors, managers, is the City Council – the Big Bad Landlord. A balance has always to be found between the forces of freedom and restriction. Both parties consist of individuals fulfilling their allotted and necessary roles. They are not so much diametrically opposed as dialectically associated. For either side to have full rein would result in chaos on the one hand and ordered sterility on the other.

Part of the success of the market, part of its wonderful achievement, is that this balance has been, on the whole, well-kept. There are the occasional skirmishes, there are areas of resentment, and recently there has been an outright battle, but this is all part of the dynamics of the place.

Flux is a part of that dynamic – from within, with the changes brought about by succeeding generations of stall-holders – and from without, imposed from time to time by the authorities. We are on the brink of such a change, for as one City Council official put it:

> There's a lot of mythologising about the market. It's one of the most valuable retail areas of the city and should pay its way. I think it should be a fold-away market. Norwich is the only city in England with such a large public space in the centre and it should be available for public events. You should have see it when we were promoted to the Premiership. People were clambering all over the stalls. It was in the way.

So, there is apprehension on both sides, as well as among the public.

**Kevin Greene** – Market Manager

Kevin is based with three others in the market office in Gladstone House in St Giles. He likes this arrangement. They can discuss any small problems that arise. Eileen, his assistant, copies interesting items for me – newspaper articles, and so on. Kevin has a round, cheery face and a friendly manner.

> Norwich Market is unique. All human life is there. It is the physical and geographical centre of Norwich. It's also unusual in that all the surrounding shops face on to it.

The tourists love it because it is antiquated, quaint, atmospheric. But people are getting used to shopping in an easy fashion and it's not pulling them in. Doing nothing isn't an option. Nor is closing it down. King Edward III granted the franchise 'in perpetuity'. But the infrastructure is old and tired. To renew all the services: water. electricity, gas, drainage, we have to move it temporarily. This is a problem. We don't want all the traders to disappear. And we've got to make sure we end up with a real market – not a civic-award winner!

It would be easy to say goodbye – but if we lose the skills and the infrastructure that supports them it would be impossible to restore. What do I think of the French Market? I think it's very good for the people of Norwich. Also, the rules are very strict so the standard is very high. I know that some of the traders object but not everyone. The Pet Stall had a good day, and the onion and garlic man bought three or four pairs of jeans. You can't prevent competition. You have to compete with it.

My background is trees, trees and the natural world. So I understand the importance of bio-diversity. We need commercial diversity in just the same way.

**Gwyn Jones** – Planning Regeneration Manager, Norwich City Council

Gwyn is gentle mannered and quietly spoken with dark, velvet eyes and brown curling hair. She is coolly professional throughout our conversation.

The market has to change, but we're trying to bring people along with us. There was the Ideas Competition in which members of the public were invited to submit their ideas. Out of this and other public consultation we came up with a design brief. There's a market consultative committee and we're in regular dialogue with the traders. The architect in charge is George Ishmael.

There are many aspects to consider: legal, financial, operational and design. We have to think long term and to find the balance between present needs and future sustainability. Of course we want to keep the best qualities of the present market – so we're looking at organised chaos.

We have to consider the kind of commodities people will be buying in twenty years time. Markets are generally in decline. The tourists do visit – partly because the market is on the tourists brochures – but they don't spend much money. That's a lot of untapped potential.

We've also done research into other cities in the UK, the US and Europe to discover what works there. We don't want to lose the custom of the poor and elderly but we have to upgrade it. We're consulting with retail specialists and market analysts – but everyone will be informed. We're not going to impose anything and the traders will know what we intend to do before anyone else.

The improvement to the Castle and the Forum has given people higher expectations. There are many practical issues to be resolved, but some sort of plan will be available to the public soon. We're trying to get funding from several sources – the City Council, Europe (but there are strings

attached to that), The East of England Development Board, English Heritage and the Heritage Lottery Fund.

The project has a high profile nationally and with Government agencies. Norwich is one of 24 cities selected to encourage a better practice of regeneration. We want to involve the community and create something modern but compatible with this historic city. We're also supported by the CABE, which is the Commission for Architecture and the Best Environment. Of course, everything depends on money.

## George Ishmael – Landscape and Planning

George has slow measured speech and a warm Lancashire accent. He has a fresh complexion, silver hair and large, grey–green lambent eyes. Like many people working in City Hall, he has to find a balance between responsibility to his employers and what may be his personal opinions.

The market occupies the biggest civic space in England. We have to change it – but there are now so many rules and regulations that it is difficult to make the changes without affecting the character of the place. The market excludes a lot of people – tall people for a start. They bang their heads. People with motorised buggies. We need to widen the aisles to accommodate them. From six feet to eleven feet. We would also like to increase the size of the stalls – from 80 square feet to 95 square feet. We would like to make the demarcation lines clear, contrasting blue brick with York stone. The market deserves good quality materials in keeping with the setting and these would be easy to clean. Ideally we would like to do it in phases – so that we don't lose too many of the traders – but that puts up the cost a lot. Also, there would be a lot of dust which would be a nuisance to remaining stall-holders. We've looked at lots of other markets – in England and elsewhere, to try to glean the best from them.

## Andy Permain – City Councillor

The market is scruffy, dirty and claustrophobic. It won't survive in its present form. There's a general sense of blight. Stalls are closing all the time. I've noticed Goldings's – the tea and coffee stall has closed. It's also a bit exclusive – stalls passed down from father to son, and so on. There's a great resistance to new ideas – they should resist the bad ones – but they resist the good ones as well. It should be a farmer's market with more stalls selling local organic produce. And there should be craft stalls – we have so many craftspeople in Norfolk. I went to a market in Seattle The traders put on a show there – a kind of entertainment. The fishmongers were juggling fish! How about that!

### 'It's like a medieval rat's nest.'

Norwich market has been radically refurbished twice in the twentieth century: in the 1930s, when the ramshackle collection of stalls was replaced with the current arrangement; and again in 1976. Despite the changes, the market remained essentially the same: a huddle, a muddle, a hotchpotch, a maze.

But there is general recognition that the market is once again much in need of refurbishment. Services like electricity and drainage have deteriorated beyond repair. General maintenance has not been what it should be. Some of the traders – and the public – sincerely believe that the Council has deliberately run the market down in order to make way for demolition.

**The market stinks of piss. There's dog shit in the aisles. Why doesn't the council do something about that? *Man with dog at public meeting.***

In addition, Norwich has undergone something of a sea-change in recent years. The new Millennium Library has set a confident tone, there is the new Castle Mall and the Chapelfield redevelopment. (It was a stroke of genius to take the huge copper bowl used for mixing chocolate from the Old Nestlé Factory and install it as a christening font in the Cathedral. A chocolate font! Baptism with the Holy Spirit and the Ghost of Chocolate past. Only Norwich could think of that!) There are other developments such as Riverside which have not been so favourably received. It was felt by some that the market needed to be upgraded in keeping with all this.

After many proposals discussed, offered (including an Ideas Competition open to the public), abandoned – mainly through lack of funds – on 18th December 2003 the City Council unveiled its three radical, innovative, and very startling designs. There was a choice between pods, waves and pyramids, made variously of concrete, metal, and plastic. A striking feature of two of the designs was that they isolated the traders from each other. There was to be a consultation period of six weeks and the final decision would be made on 16th February. The council's determination was clear:

**As an administration, we are committed to see this project happen and it is going to happen. No change is not an option as far as we are concerned. *Brian Watkins, Council's Executive Member for Enterprise, 18th December 2003***

Or was it?

The designs are not set in stone and we will take all views into account. *Ian Couzens, Leader of the City Council, 18th December 2003*

One member of the council expressed his enthusiasm:

I favour a modern 'wow' design. Something new for the city. The next step in the Renaissance of Norwich. *Derek Wood, City Council Executive*

But the public felt differently:

These plans are just a joke – like Riverside. You should give the traders something to be proud of! *Man with dog at public meeting*

The traders had not even had a preview of the designs, never mind been consulted. There have been no talks or debates with the traders since June. The council is forgetting the human aspect. We are talking about people's livelihoods. *Ron Macleish, Events Stall*

Traders offered their own idea for a new design:

The market needs cleaning up. I think it should be circular with the food stalls in the middle like a central plaza, the other stalls radiating out like spokes in a wheel. *David Ridgeway, Bags and Belts*

The market needs a revamp. People avoid it because it's dirty and run-down. But we need to keep the variety. We could also do with a plan or stall guide. *John Ellis, Bookstall*

The traders were invited individually to make an appointment to see a certain gentleman at City Hall and were then told that it was a *fait accompli*. They would be evicted *en masse* at the end of December 2004 and invited to apply for one of the much reduced – and undoubtedly more expensive – number of stalls to be up and running by October 2005. The traders were resigned and dispirited.

If it 'appen, it 'appen. There's nothing you can do about it. They'll never do it properly anyway. Greed. In 1976 they crammed in as many stalls as they could. They want it to be like continental olde worlde. The only way you can do that is by leaving it alone. *Alex Pond*

But the City Council had not got the measure of things; they had seriously misread the situation – not only in the designs, but in the unjust and shabby treatment of the traders, and in what they viewed as 'modern expectations of an attractive retail environment'. Orchestrated by the Eastern Counties Newspapers, there was immediate uproar – from the public, the traders, as well as official bodies like the Norwich Society and the Inner City Forum. The plans were variously described as 'terrifyingly awful', 'horrible', 'ghastly', 'dreary', 'sterile'.

The designs are simply rubbish, lacking in just about any form of imagination, style, character, inspiration or understanding of what a market should be. *Martin Kentish, EDP, 17th January 2004*

I think only stall-holders and Norfolk people who use the market should have any say on its future. What percentage of people who work for the City Council use the market? *H. J. Fairhead, EDP, 10th January 2004*

The brightly coloured canopies, the maze of traders, the dizzying, off-balance sensation of being perpetually 'on the huh', the Hoover stall – the market is an eccentric wonder in a world of bland, homogenous retailers … For many, rubbing up against shoppers near the cheese stall as they try to purchase a decent blue-veiner is the closest they ever get to full sex … Simply by being timeless, the market-place is, and for ever will be, contemporary. It is already so unique that it defies redesign. The Council needs to be told. The designs are awful. You're wrong. It's a bad idea. Listen to the people. Don't do it. *Karl Minns, Evening News, 23rd January 2004*

Have you ever heard of a clean market? It's not the nature of the beast. *Jennifer Edmonds, Family History Shop*

I'd like it to stay the same, but it should be cleaned up. It's like a medieval rat's nest. *Paul Durrant*

These designs alienate the people from the market, the 'hands-on' feeling of being part of a wonderful jumble of colours, smells and sounds. *Victoria Allen, EDP, 24th January 2004*

I love to take visitors there. Even in its dilapidated state, it has a charm that brings a smile to their faces. It's the bright stripes of the roofs, the open stalls, its inviting air, with old-fashioned charm and cheery, helpful traders. *Olga Sinclair, EDP, 26th January 2004*

*Markets are organic. They need to be chaotic, crowded and lively and Norwich Market stands in wonderful contrast to the sterility, conformity and predictability of modern shops. H. Williams, EDP, 26th January 2004*

Almost unanimously, apart from one correspondent who wanted to 'bulldoze the lot into the Wensum', people were overwhelmingly in favour of a fourth option: refurbish, replenish, restore, renew, but retain the essential character.

*If it aint broke, don't fix it. It will be throwing the baby out with the bath water. Jeremy Crisp, EDP, 8th January 2004*

*We have been shopping at the market for 30 years and would hate to see it turned into an American theme park or painted toy town. Judy Muskett, EDP, 20th January 2004*

But the council remained adamant:

*Norwich Council last night refused to abandon the three controversial designs drawn up to dramatically transform the city's historic market-place. EDP, 20th January 2004*

So did the public:

*This is a bad decision and one that smacks of Big Brother. Mike Hull, 21st January 2004*

*The plastic or crinkly tin being suggested for the awnings are no substitute for canvas or cloth. And the colours are no good. They simply don't age gracefully and the water runs off too fast. Pile it high and sell it cheap, with all the emphasis on the goods, a great buzz, crowds and sense of fun. This is what people come for. Not a dreary, sterile, municipal interpretation of an age-old theme. Michael Innes, Architect*

*If we are going for open heart surgery, then it's most important that the patient survives. John Loveday, 13th January 2004*

*It would be like modernising the casbahs of North Africa. Bernard Hill*

Word spread. On 23rd January the *Eastern Daily Press* reported:

*Communities from across the world have joined forces to oppose the controversial plans to transform Norwich Market. The Norfolk and Norwich family, an organisation made up of all towns and cities bearing the same name world-wide, has said the market should be left mainly as it is.*

One person even saw the perverse designs as part of a cunning plot:

**The Council has put forward plans they know no one will like. With this result, they will say that people don't want any change, so we'll just give it a coat of paint and perhaps, if we can afford it, some new litter bins. M. J. Sankey, EDP, 2nd March 2004**

It was an unprecedented outcry. There were public meetings. The traders organised a petition which soon had over 12,000 signatures; a local solicitor offered his services to the traders for free which they accepted to great effect. From as far away as Las Vegas people sent in their protests. On Valentine's Day there was a 'Hands around the Market' demonstration.

But by then it was almost unnecessary. The Council's resolve had slowly been crumbling and now they backed down altogether. They would give the people of Norwich what they wanted. The market as it is. The promise was made at a public meeting and announced in a headline in the Evening News on 26th January.

## COUNCIL CHIEF ADMITS DEFEAT
**We are finding out what the stall-holders and people of Norwich want and will try our best to fulfill their wishes. Hereward Cook, Deputy Leader of the Council.**

So why? What is it about this flimsy structure, this hickory-dickory hotchpotch, that inspires so much passion? Like the Castle and the Cathedral, the Provision Market is a legacy of the Norman Conquest, enduring though fragile, and no less revered. It is not only in the affections of the people, but in their collective memory, but in some way it goes deep into their psyche. The market is more than just a place. It is a living organism, made of hands, hearts, faces, voices, memories, ghosts. It is an expression of spirit, of soul, of character.

Not the least of this is that it is the heart of Norwich in more than a physical sense: it is a place of cheerfulness, acceptance and kindness.

**We contribute to the social life of many of the elderly who are able to meet friends for a cup of tea for 28 pence and enjoy the market banter. Kate Claxton, Ruby's Teas**

The new plans promised to 'incorporate public art'. But in this City of Culture, the market is public art, our most expressive, most shared and accessible cultural artefact. It has developed over the centuries and cannot be deliberately engendered. It is organic and authentic, the opposite of artificial and imposed. People know this. And it is entirely in keeping with the radical, nonconformist spirit of Norwich that the people rose up to protect it.

It is not only our voice that was heard, but the voices echoing down the years.

**'When something like this dies, it dies inside yourself. The people will be in mourning.'**

Since human beings formed the first communities, the market-place has been as essential to physical survival as the church is to the spiritual. It is a place where people naturally congregate, interact, exchange. Every village and town would have had one, in some form or another.

It's purpose has not been exclusively commercial: it is here that romances were kindled, friendships forged, punishments inflicted, laws proclaimed. It is a place of collective, as well as individual, emotion. One of the most spectacular scenes since VE day must have been on the sunny evening of 10th May 2004 when more than 50,000 people gathered to celebrate Norwich City Football team's promotion to the Premiership. Such joy, such excitement, such green-and-yellow rapture, was a wonder to behold. The Bishop was there, trying to get a share of the action for God. 'God must be on your side, the sun has come out,' he told the crowd. 'You can come to the Cathedral and pray for your team any time.' Not only the market-place, the castle mound itself was overwhelmed with the clamouring, cheering, chanting crowd.

But the market has lost its essential nature. We could get by without it. The ancient imperative that binds past and future together is being gradually loosened and we have to ask ouselves why it is that people are so attached to what some regard as an antiquated, clapped-out anachronism.

Part of the answer, I believe, lies in Norwich's history: radical, individualistic, nonconformist. St Julian of Norwich, Robert Kett, Elizabeth Fry, George Borrow, Harriet Martineau, are some of the individuals who have marked this progress. (It is perhaps no coincidence that Philip Pullman, the celebrated author of the *His Dark Materials* trilogy, who has taken a stand against the whole established church, was born here.)

This spirit somehow remains defiant against the ravages of the retail experts, who would like to reduce us all to manageable and predictable consumer units, Castle Mall is an example of that, as are the endless and uniformly unattractive out-of-town shopping developments. Cities need gloss and glamour, but scruffiness, and idiosyncrasy also add spice. The contrast itself is energising.

**Where else in England do you get a proper market like this? And they want to turn it into another piece of real estate. No! We've got enough real estate. Only one market. Mark Oxley**

The corporate vision has a very wide sweep, and in some places the battle is well and truly lost. Les Halles in Paris has been replaced by a modern shopping centre. Raymond Mason, an artist, said of this: 'it was a place of joy, a place of tears. In truth, the Halles Centralles market was the last image of the Natural in the City. It is now a Paradise Lost.' Another commentator in a Sunday newspaper said: 'on a busy weekend, Covent Garden now looks like nothing so much as the departure lounge at Gatwick airport in the middle of an air-traffic-controller strike, full to bursting with sullen visitors longing for a sense of being somewhere special.'

Norwich market is somewhere special. Sullen it ain't.

So what of the future? Some people think that the market has to adapt to changing requirements, as indeed it has always done.

**It should really be a farmer's market, promoting all the wonderful food produced in Norfolk.** *Brian Pickering, Pickering's Sausage Stall*

**There ought to be more clothing here. More crafts. A bit more of Camden Lock about it.** *Isabel Chapman, Vintage Clothing*

But the issues lie deeper than this. Although no longer essential for our practical survival, Norwich Market is a link with a more authentic history. There is a continuity and an expression of communal identity that we value and recognise. This is why the protest against a severance of that was so powerful, and the sense of loss acute.

**When something like this dies, it dies inside yourself. The people will be in mourning.** *Gilles Bourlet*

Some change to the physical fabric is necessary in order to preserve that continuity – but by far the biggest threat to its future is in the willingness of the new generation to carry things forward. They too have different expectations. A willingness to work hard in all weathers, against fiercer competition, may not be one of them.

Within ten years it will all be gone. The shops are killing it off. It's untidy now and the young ones don't come here. We'll end up with just a few stalls, like on the continent. *Roy Anderson, Menswear*

I've been here 42 years. It's 3.50 now. We should be mobbed at this time. We used to come down here and have a cup of tea at eight in the morning – we didn't get another till five o'clock we were so busy. Would you work here? *Anonymous trader of fruit and veg*

I like to imagine the market in the days of the old shoe factories. In those days, people would flood into the market after work. That's all gone now. *Gareth Butcher, Herbs and Spices*

I get anxious sometimes for the future of the market. Politicians won't recognise the needs of such a place, and some of the traders are their own worst enemies. They want to do things the way they've done them for twenty years. But everything changes. Everything moves on. *Alan Trower, Cheeseman*

My son will do something different. He has a first-class honours degree. *Neil Hume, City Scenters*

No, I don't really want my children to do this. I'd like something better for them. Electronics or something. *John Kett, Roots and Fruits*

No, I don't want my children to work here. I want them to be professional. *Richard Anderson, Menswear*

I'd be happy to see my kids take over. They're three and eight years old. But my wife wants them to be professional people. It's a hard life, you see. *Alex Pond*

Two voices struck a note of optimism:

I've got three children, one seven year old, and twins of four and a half. I'd like them to take over eventually. *Ian Woods, Jewellery*

I'd like the stall to go on to the next generation. I've no regrets. *Miriam Bowgen, Cary's Flower Stall*

## 'I love the Market. It's the heart of Norwich. Absolutely beating.'

Norwich Market is a much less sensational place than it used to be. We no longer have public hangings and floggings and freak shows. The pigeons and starlings are not so spectacular as the cheetahs and elephants that were once paraded there. At election times, we don't line up to throw the cobbles we have torn from the road as they did in the eighteenth century 'when many a head was cracked'. We don't burn the books we have plundered from the churches as they did in the seventeenth century. Also, because it is no longer available as an open space, we seldom see the grand civic festivities of the past, such as the 10,000 children that assembled there on Queen Victoria's Jubilee, nor the great crowds that gathered on VE day. The crockery sellers don't even smash their crockery in mock exasperation because they 'cannot raise nine pence for it'.

Whatever happens, I doubt if anyone will take up the suggestion of a Russian diplomat in 1968, on surveying the market-place from City Hall, that it would be much better as 'a sort of Trafalgar Square'. And we don't have to undertake the drastic demolition they had to do to accommodate the market in its present size when many old lanes, inns and yards of ancient Norwich (including some of the eighteen public houses there were then) had to go. In 1991 Janet Sillett declared that the City Council will never 'yuppify, gentrify, or continentalise Norwich Market'. Whatever they do, the market has evolved around people, not planners, and reflects the individuality of human beings. It also reflects much of the Norfolk character – individualistic, radical, nonconformist, socially inclusive. It will take more than the planners to eradicate that.

The sounds emanating from 'this babel with its armageddon of shouts, cries and calls, this bedlam of noise', are more subdued now, the manners more tempered. But it is still the psychological centre of Norwich, its hub and its heart. It is a never-ending story. For every fragment in these pages, there are thousands more. I'd like to think that reading this will bring them closer to the tips of tongues; maybe even to the ends of pens.

I love the Market. It's the heart of Norwich. Absolutely beating. *Phillip Browne*